Speed Training

Speed Training

Systems for Learning
in Times of Rapid Change

Jim Stewart

BCA

LONDON   NEW YORK   SYDNEY   TORONTO

First published in 1993

This edition published 1993 by BCA by arrangement with Kogan
Page Limited

CN 4470

Typeset by Saxon Graphics Ltd, Derby
Printed and bound in Great Britain by Clays Ltd, St Ives plc

For my son Paul, in recognition of the opportunities for practice which he provided, and with thanks for his suggestions and comments

Contents

Preface

Coping with rapid and continuous change is the biggest challenge facing managers in organizations today, and this situation is likely to continue. The *speed* of change is increasing, too: new equipment, new policies, new procedures, new products, new customers... and in the future, corporate success will depend on each manager's ability to co-ordinate and implement this change.

At the same time, we are witnessing an increased emphasis on performance and accountability within companies: in particular, a *manager*'s performance is judged by his or her *staff*'s performance.

Thankfully, it is now well known that staff will not perform at their best unless they are trained and developed. Managers are, therefore, finding themselves increasingly responsible for the training of their staff, whether or not an organization has a training department.

With this increasing demand for new knowledge and skills, the amount of time spent on training will grow in the future, so managers need clear, straightforward guidelines on the most appropriate, and most time-saving training methods. SPEEDTRAINING: SYSTEMS FOR LEARNING IN TIMES OF RAPID CHANGE has been written in response to this demand, and I am convinced that the new

SHAPE system presented here will assure the rapid and co-ordinated training of your staff.

Jim Stewart
Nottingham Trent Business School
May 1993

1 SHAPE Employee Performance

1 SHAPE Employee Performance

Introduction

This book is about training and development. It is not, though, written for training specialists. It is a simple, clear path through the training maze written for managers and supervisors.

Think about what being a manager means.

As a manager you are not employed to sell or to make or to process or to provide whatever your organization exists to provide. Your job is to *manage* the selling or the making or the processing or the service provision. You are accountable for the efficiency and effectiveness of the activities involved in those functions, and for ensuring that those activities contribute to the organization achieving its objectives.

Efficiency and effectiveness depend on how well resources are used. You are accountable as a manager for the resources allocated to you: your job essentially involves getting the best out of those resources. The resources you have generally fall into one of four types:

- Money
- Materials

- Equipment
- People.

The most critical resource is *people*. It is your staff who directly use the other resources to sell or to make or to process or to provide a service. How well the resources of money, materials and equipment are used depends upon the resource of people. So, as a manager you must ensure you get the best out of your staff otherwise you will not get the best out of your other resources. You will not achieve maximum efficiency and effectiveness.

Managers and Training and Development

Your key accountability as a manager then, is managing your staff. Your performance is judged by their performance. Your staff, though, will not perform at their best unless they are *trained* and *developed*. People cannot achieve excellent performance unless they have the required ability: they must be trained.

Since you are accountable for the performance of your staff, and their performance depends on how well they are trained and developed, you are as a manager responsible for their training. Your organization may have a training department with specialist trainers, but the training of your staff is not their responsibility – it is yours, because you are responsible for your staff as a resource and for their performance.

Manager contributions

As a manager you play a critical role in training your staff. The contributions you can make include the following:

- **Identifying needs.** You are closest to your staff; you

know how they perform on a day-to-day basis. You are therefore the person best placed to identify their training needs.

■ **Selecting trainees.** If you do have a training department which provides central courses it is your job to decide which of your staff goes on which course. This follows from identifying their needs.

■ **Setting standards.** The purpose of training and development is to enable individuals to perform at the required standard; the standard, though, has to be specified. You are accountable for and control the performance of your department; you must therefore set the standards.

■ **Assessing results.** The results of training have to be assessed. This means assessing the performance of individuals against the standards to check the value of training. Determining whether staff are performing satisfactorily is obviously part of your job; you must therefore assess the results of training.

There is one activity missing from this list. It is actually *providing* the training to your staff. Whether or not you have a training department which offers courses, providing the training yourself within your department is always an option you must consider.

The Importance of On-the-Job Training

Providing training yourself within the department is known as 'on-the-job training'. This form of training has many advantages, including the fact that it is:

■ Quicker to organize

■ Cheaper to deliver

- More relevant to real needs
- Immediately applied in work
- Within your direct control.

It is well recognized by both managers and trainers that the further away from the job that training occurs the less effective it is likely to be. Conversely, the closer to the job training happens the more effective it will be. On-the-job training is likely, therefore, in most cases to be the preferred option.

There is another and increasingly important reason why this is the case. It is simply that the *speed of change* is increasing. Change is now commonplace in most organizations. New equipment, new policies, new procedures, new products, new customers, etc – the list is endless. The biggest challenge facing you and your staff is probably coping with change, and to cope successfully requires training and development. Staff have to learn new knowledge and skills to deal with the consequences of change. The amount of time you spend on training your staff because of change could grow and grow in the future. Using the SHAPE system for speedtraining will help you to control this tendency.

The Purpose and Use of SHAPE for Speedtraining

Given the growing importance of training and development, the primary purpose of the SHAPE system is to help you to manage the rapid and coordinated training of your staff.

To be a successful manager now and in the future requires you to be effective in managing the training of your staff. The SHAPE system of training explains how to achieve that. It is a training system which is based on sound training practice. The basis of SHAPE is the training cycle which is shown in Figure 1.1.

Figure 1.1 *The training cycle*

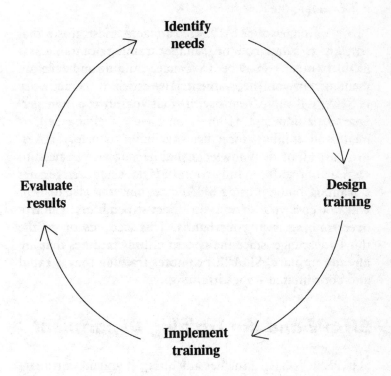

SHAPE and the Training Cycle

The training cycle simplifies the activities which are involved in managing training and development; it represents a summary of those activities. SHAPE provides an easy-to-remember acronym which encompasses the same activities. The meaning of the acronym is:

S = Set Performance Standards
H = Harness Your Resources
A = Assess Individual and Team Needs
P = Plan, Prepare and Present Training
E = Evaluate the Results.

The advantages of SHAPE are threefold. First, it is a system which is designed for managers rather than trainers. It enables you as a manager to manage training and development within your department. The order of the activities in SHAPE is more in line with what you do as a manager. Second, it does not assume you have a training department and training specialists available to help. SHAPE provides all of the knowledge and techniques you need to ensure your staff are fully trained. It does not even require a training budget: using SHAPE within your department will not cost you a penny in direct expenditure. Control over training is in your hands. This leads us on to the third advantage: since the system utilizes facilities that are already in place, SHAPE promotes training that is rapid and coordinated – speedtraining.

SHAPE and the Training Department

SHAPE does have a further advantage if you are fortunate enough to work in an organization with a training department. Being familiar with SHAPE and applying some of the elements from the system will enable you to get the best for your section out of the training department. SHAPE achieves this by allowing you to do the following:

■ Identify needs accurately

■ Prepare and control training plans

■ Talk 'the language' of training with specialists

■ Assess courses and services provided by the training department

- Evaluate the results of training
- Actively manage training and development in your section.

Achieving all of these in practice will ensure that you achieve the best possible returns from your training budget and use of your training department.

Practical Benefits of SHAPE

Whether you utilize SHAPE fully through on-the-job training or only in part, you can expect some real and practical benefits. Those which are most important in terms of the performance of your section are:

- Reduced wastage of materials
- Reduced errors and re-work
- Reduced learning times for new staff
- Increased quality
- Increased flexibility of staff
- Increased individual performance.

Each of these benefits will have two effects. First, they will *reduce costs*. Second, they will *increase productivity*, ie, the amount of work done by the same number of people in the same amount of time. Both of these effects will in turn *improve* the performance of your department, and continued application of SHAPE in response to change will ensure continued improvement.

The benefits listed are direct and easily measured. They come from ensuring your staff have the required *ability*. Using SHAPE, though, will have additional benefits. Because they are able and because they are being trained when required, your staff will be more *motivated*. A higher level of motivation also brings benefits which are perhaps more indirect but still measurable. You can therefore also expect the following additional benefits from utilizing SHAPE:

- Reduced accidents
- Reduced absenteeism
- Reduced labour turnover
- Reduced complaints from staff and customers.

Each of these benefits will reduce costs and increase productivity and, therefore, improve the overall performance of your department.

If you do not utilize SHAPE, you can expect the opposite: those measures you want to reduce will increase and those you want to increase will reduce. You cannot afford *not* to use SHAPE.

Speedtraining through SHAPE

The final and perhaps most important benefit of SHAPE is reflected in the title of this book: *Speedtraining*. The SHAPE acronym represents an overall approach to training from a manager's viewpoint. Applying the principles in practice means saving your time and saving the time of your staff. SHAPE provides the means of 'speeding up' the whole process of training and development, hence the title *Speedtraining*.

This point permeates all of the elements of SHAPE. Each part of SHAPE contains systems for dealing with each of the steps required for successful and effective training. Every element within SHAPE is designed with the explicit aim of making the job of training easier, quicker and more flexible. This means that whenever you are faced with a training problem, you have a system available which enables you to identify and implement an effective solution very quickly. Thus, *Speedtraining* is an accurate description of what you will achieve by utilizing SHAPE.

Because of this ability to respond quickly and speedily by providing appropriate training, you will be in a strong position to manage change effectively. Therefore the single most important benefit to you of speedtraining through SHAPE is the advantage it gives you in coping with a changing and competitive business environment.

The Purpose of this Book

The purpose of this book is to enable you to achieve the benefits of training and development. It achieves that purpose by explaining the SHAPE system. Each element of SHAPE is given a separate chapter. The final chapter concludes the book with some advice on getting the best out of the total SHAPE system.

Most chapters explaining SHAPE have the following features:

■ An introductory section

■ Examples of applying techniques

■ Suggested formats and aids for use in practice

■ Completed examples of formats and aids

■ Hints on getting the best out of each element of SHAPE

■ An example case study illustrating application in practice

■ A summary and checklists.

All of these features will help you understand and use SHAPE. Remember, though, that it is only by putting the system into practice that you will gain the benefits.

One final point. The book is aimed at and written for managers and supervisors from any industry or sector of the economy. It does not matter whether you work in manufacturing, retail, local government or wherever: SHAPE will work for you. Terminology, though, does vary. I use the words 'section' and 'department' to mean the same; you may use a different word. The meaning is simply that part of the organization for which you are responsible.

2 S: Set Performance Standards

2 S: Set Performance Standards

Introduction

The starting point in the SHAPE system is to Set Standards. These standards must be related to performance. The whole purpose of staff training is to enable individuals to perform to the required standards, which in turn enables your section to achieve its objectives.

Levels of Performance

Performance standards have to be set at three related levels:

- The section
- The team
- The individual.

There is in fact a fourth level: the organization. Standards at all other levels are derived from the performance requirements of the organization. You are unlikely to have great influence at that level. You must, though, take organizational requirements as your starting point in formulating standards and objectives at the three levels within your area of control.

Three Important Ideas

In setting performance standards you need to consider three related ideas:

■ **Performance.** This idea concerns what needs to be *done*. It defines the actions and activities which have to be undertaken. In simple terms, performance is the same as *tasks* that are carried out in your section.

■ **Objectives.** Objectives differ from the idea of performance in that they describe what is *achieved* by the performance. Performance is a *process*. Objectives are the *outputs* which are achieved by the process of performance.

■ **Standards.** Standards can be applied to both performance and objectives. The idea of standards is essentially to do with *criteria*. They specify how well performance should be undertaken and how well objectives should be achieved. As criteria, standards are concerned with *measures* of performance and objectives. These measures normally focus on *quantity* and *quality*.

These ideas are used in various ways in each of the three levels of the section, the team and the individual. To illustrate what the ideas mean in practice, Figure 2.1 provides an example of how they apply to the everyday activity of making a pot of tea.

Figure 2.1 *Objectives, performance and standards*

Objective	A pot of freshly brewed tea sufficient for four people is available.
Performance	Fill electric kettle and boil water. Place two tea bags in teapot. Pour water when boiling from kettle into teapot until teapot full. Stir tea in pot, cover and leave to stand.
Standards	Temperature of tea is between X and Y degrees centigrade. Operation takes no longer than Z minutes. Tea is left to stand for two minutes before pouring.

The Section Level

It is not possible for an outsider to provide performance standards for your section; only you and your manager can do that. To do so, you have to think through the answers to a number of questions.

Mission Statement

The starting point is to consider the 'mission' of your section. The idea of a mission is quite simple: it means the primary purpose of your section. In brief, it means asking what the section exists to *do* and what it exists to *achieve*. Answering those two questions will enable you to write a mission statement. This statement describes a mixture of the performance and objectives of your section.

To produce a mission statement for your section, think about and produce answers to the following questions:

■ Why does your section exist?

■ What is the *unique* contribution of your section to the organization?

■ What would be the consequences of your section *not* existing?

■ What does ultimate success for your section look like?

A very important starting point in addressing these questions is the corporate mission of your organization. Your section and its work will in some way relate to the overall mission and goals of the total organization. The answers you arrive at to the questions for your section must reflect and flow from the corporate mission. The corporate mission statement itself will be very helpful in answering the questions, which will, in turn, give you the information you need to write your mission statement. The mission statement itself must have certain characteristics, especially the following:

■ A 'synthesis' of vision and realism

■ A statement of the achievable

■ Brief and to the point

■ Clear and memorable.

Figure 2.2 provides some examples of mission statements to show the practical meaning of these characteristics.

Figure 2.2 *Examples of mission statements*

A – Sales
'To provide the highest standard of customer service to ensure continuous growth of new and repeat business'.

B – Production
'To produce the highest quality (widget) to specifications and within time and cost budgets'.

C – Administration
'To ensure an efficient and effective service to client departments across the range of administrative functions for which the section is responsible'.

Notes
1) These statements assume a single-function section.
2) Where no responsibility or accountability exists, no mention is made in the statement. None of the examples has responsibility for profit so it does not form part of the statement. Examples A and C are not accountable for costs and so these too are ignored in the statements.

Key Results Areas

Once you have a mission statement you will find it easier to move on to the next stage, which is to identify your key results.

Key results for your section will fall into a number of different areas. These are termed 'Key Results Areas', or KRAs. Going through the process of producing your mission statement will have highlighted what your particular

KRAs are likely to be. However, you do need to think about and list them separately to make sure none are overlooked.

KRAs reflect your individual performance requirements as a manager. Put simply, your job is to ensure that your section achieves its purpose; therefore your personal performance is inextricably linked to that of your section and vice-versa.

The idea of KRA is to focus attention on the *critical* or *important* or *priority* results that you and your section have to achieve. Not all of your results areas will be critical or *key*. Some common KRAs for managers are given in the following list, but you and your manager have to determine which are relevant to your situation:

- Marketing and sales

- Finance and costs

- Profitability

- Productivity and output

- Human resources

- Ideas and innovation

- Special projects.

To demonstrate how KRAs relate to mission statements, Figure 2.3 shows a set of KRAs for one of the statements taken from Figure 2.2.

Objectives

Once you have your KRAs agreed, you are in a position to formulate relevant and usable objectives. Remember that objectives are *output*-orientated. In effect, objectives describe the *conditions* which are to be created by the work of your section.

Figure 2.3 *Examples of key results areas*

'To provide the highest standard of customer service to ensure continuous growth of new and repeat business'.

Key Results Areas
1. Marketing and sales
2. Ideas and innovation
3. Human resources
4. Special projects.

Note
Human resources is, by definition, a standard KRA for any section manager.

Objectives should have certain characteristics. These are conveniently summarized by the acronym SMART. The meaning of SMART is:

■ **S = Specific.** This means that generalized statements should be avoided. Phrases such as, 'To maximize profits' are too general to be useful and therefore objectives need to relate to precise and specific activities within individual KRAs.

■ **M = Measurable.** Another problem with 'maximize profits' is that nobody knows whether or not it has been achieved – it is not measurable. Objectives need to contain measures which can be assessed.

■ **A = Achievable.** Clear objectives are motivating. Progress towards them can be monitored and positive feedback gained. This will not be the case if the objective is too ambitious. For example, 'Increase profits by 200 per cent' is an objective which is likely to be ignored.

■ **R = Realistic.** That last statement could, though, be inaccurate. Objectives have to be realistic in the light of given circumstances. In some circumstances, 'Increase profits by 200 per cent' may be achievable and therefore realistic. Realism also works the other way. Objectives should be challenging and not capable of achievement without effort.

■ **T = Time-bound.** The final characteristic is that objectives should be given a time frame. This defines the time-scale within which the objective will be achieved. The usual ways of expressing this characteristic are either to set a target day, eg, 'By the end of March 1994', or to define the required time period, eg, 'Within the financial year'.

Types of Objective

Objectives can usually be classified into two different types:

■ Standard and ongoing

■ Non-recurring.

You will have a number of each or both of these types for each of your KRAs. Non-recurring objectives will obviously predominate in the KRA of 'special projects'. Indeed, it is likely that this KRA will contain exclusively non-recurring objectives: your special projects will be different each year. Standard and ongoing objectives are those which always form part of your performance requirements, for example, something like the following:

■ Increase sales turnover by 15 per cent (Sales)

■ Increase unit output per operator by 5 per cent (Production)

■ Increase throughput of sales invoices by 10 per cent (Data Processing)

■ Decrease amount of re-work through errors by 12 per cent (Typing Pool).

These examples illustrate how your personal performance and that of your section are in reality the same. The objectives can only be achieved by your *section* and are measures of its performance, but *you* will be personally accountable for their achievements.

KRAs other than special projects can also have non-recurring objectives. For example, in sales, certain products may be emphasized in some years and not others. In production, the level of scrap as a cost item may be emphasized in one time period and the breakdown of machinery in another. All of these items are likely to be subject to standard ongoing objectives but may come in for special attention with non-recurring objectives being attached to them at different points in time.

How objectives relate to KRAs and what they look like in practice are illustrated in Figure 2.4. The objectives given are derived from a KRA selected from Figure 2.3.

A final point about objectives. You will notice that the examples given above and in Figure 2.4 conform to the SMART acronym. This means that they contain measurable elements. These elements are in fact specifications of STANDARDS.

Standards

As we saw earlier, standards are to do with criteria which specify how well something is to be done or achieved. In that sense, therefore, the measurable elements of the objectives are indeed standards.

The use of standards in relation to *performance* is, though, slightly different from that for objectives. Standards for performance have the following two characteristics:

Figure 2.4 *Examples of objectives*

KRA – Marketing and Sales

1. Increase number of regular telephone contacts with new customers by 10 per cent per month within next three months.
2. Re-activate 12 established but dormant customers within six months.
3. Secure three orders per month for new product X from new or established customers for next nine months.
4. Produce an increase of 15 per cent over 199X figures on sales turnover from new and established customers in current year.
5. Compile a list of potential new customers in geographic area ABC by end of half-year.

- More specific and detailed

- Define more durable and *absolute* measurements.

What this means in practice is first, that performance standards are required for individual tasks and activities. Objectives are normally formulated for KRAs. Each KRA, though, incorporates and requires a multitude of tasks to be undertaken. Each of these tasks has to have a defined standard.

Second, standards for these tasks do not necessarily change within regular time periods, unlike those for objectives.

Specifying Standards

Standards usually specify measures of performance in two areas. Some examples within each area are:

Quantity	Number of units	Produced
		Sold
		Processed
		Repaired
	Time taken	Per unit
		Per batch
		Per activity
		Per task
Quality	Number of errors	Per unit of work
		Per time period
		Wastage rates
		Amount of re-work
	Number of complaints	Per time period
		Per customer
		Per staff member

It is difficult to be precise about standards in this book since the focus of standards varies considerably between different industries and types of organizations. The critical point is that standards *exist* and that they are *measurable* in terms of quantity and quality. Some examples of standards as they apply to common tasks are given in Figure 2.5 to further illustrate their use in practice.

Summary

The use of mission statements, KRAs, objectives and standards is all part of managing your section. They all enable you to do your job efficiently and effectively. Certainly, without the clear picture of performance requirements which emerges from developing these ideas in practice it is impossible to get the most out of your staff through training and development. The purpose of training is to enable performance requirements to be met; that cannot happen without those requirements being known and specified. One particular and specific application of the ideas of objectives and standards to training purposes is in formulating training objectives. This application is explained in the final section of this chapter.

Figure 2.5 *Examples of standards*

1. Typing   Produce minimum of 12 standard pieces of work per day with no more than three errors per piece of work.

2. Production   Complete finishing operation on X product at the rate of 200 per shift with a reject rate of less than 5 per cent.

3. Administration   Process six invoices per hour with each filed correctly by the end of the working day.

4. Sales   Contact six new customers per week by telephone with a minimum of two being converted to personal visits.

 SPEEDTRAINING TIP

Use available information, for instance bonus or commission schemes, to specify standards. This will save you the time and effort needed to produce specifications.

The Team Level

The benefits of having a clear picture of performance requirements becomes apparent when you move on to the team and individual level. Just as the work of your section flows from the goals and objectives of the organization, so the work of your teams and individual members of staff flows from the goals and objectives of your section.

Analysing and specifying performance requirements for the teams in your section involves a very simple three-stage process:

■ **Identify the teams.** This is an obvious but necessary first step. Work teams consist of collections of individuals who share a clear, common goal and who are mutually interdependent for achievement of their tasks. Obviously, this is true of your whole section, but there will be naturally occurring groups of employees who, because of the nature of their work, constitute teams within the section. For example:

- Sales staff, and
- Administration staff; or

- Production staff, and
- Maintenance staff; or

- Wages staff, and
- Invoice staff.

■ **Determine KRAs.** From the analysis carried out for the section it will be a simple matter to determine KRAs for each team. Some section-level KRAs will naturally fall to particular teams, eg, marketing and sales to the sales team, or productivity and output to the production team. However, each team will have KRAs of their own which are not the same as the section KRAs but which derive from them.

■ **Set objectives and standards.** From the KRAs for each

team will flow their particular objectives and standards. The way these are expressed is the same as for the section level. As with KRAs, some objectives will be those set for the section and some will be derived from section objectives.

There are two important provisos to this process. The first is that you obviously need to involve team leaders and indeed members of the teams, in determining KRAs, objectives and standards. Second, you may well have ad hoc teams working for fixed periods of time. This will certainly be the case in relation to special projects. An example would be a team created to implement a new ordering and billing system which draws on both sales and admin staff for its membership. You will need to engage in the same process for those teams.

CASE STUDY 1

Mike is an advertising sales manager working for a provincial newspaper. He is experienced in the job and manages a professional team of sales representatives and related staff. However, increasing competition from rival 'Free Distribution' papers and local commercial radio stations was beginning to have serious effects on the bottom-line performance of his department. This in turn was causing the various teams in his department to question each other's contribution. There was growing confusion and argument over who was directly responsible for each part of the service provided to customers and increasing resentment caused by staff accusing each other of 'not pulling their weight'.

Mike's response to this situation was to establish clarity in the department's operations by applying the principles of setting standards. Working with section heads responsible for sales, advertising design and

---

copy-writing, Mike established a department mission and identified key results areas and objectives for each section. He then worked separately with each section head to set performance standards for each job within the department. He agreed personal performance objectives with each section head and insisted they do the same for each member of their staff. The results of this work were communicated to all members of the department.

The effects were immediately apparent. Everyone in the department became clear about their individual role and their performance is now easily monitored. Required changes in objectives are now more easily and more quickly identified and communicated. Customer service continues to improve and the department is able to clearly demonstrate the added value it brings to the business. Staff are highly motivated and ready and able to handle the competition.

The Individual Level

The final level at which you need to determine performance requirements is the individual level. This level is perhaps the most critical, certainly for training purposes. It is also important because if requirements are not met at this level, they will not be met by teams or the section.

There are two separate elements to the individual level:

- Core performance requirements
- Personal performance requirements.

Each element needs to be set in the context of section- and team-level performance requirements. The difference between the two elements is explained below.

Core Performance Requirements

This element does not in fact focus on individuals. The focus is rather on each of the different jobs or positions in your section.

As a manager you are responsible for a group of staff who are engaged in a range of activities. The activities are grouped together into 'jobs' or 'occupations'. These jobs exist outside of the particular individuals who currently perform them. Each job in your section needs to have defined performance standards; the standards associated with the job are the 'core performance requirements'. No matter which particular individual occupies the job, they will need to meet the defined standards in carrying out the job. If you have a number of individuals doing the same job, eg, a group of sales representatives or a group of production operatives or a group of clerical assistants, each and every individual will be required to meet the same standard.

Experienced Worker Standard

What these standards are is for you as the manager to determine. Standards for some jobs may be specified by the organization, others may be partly specified through bonus or commission systems. You may be able to call in expertise such as work study specialists to help you define standards. One useful idea to help you is that of *'experienced worker standard'*, known as EWS.

EWS means exactly what it says: it is the standard of performance achieved by an experienced worker. To set the core performance requirements, simply study and analyse the performance achieved by an experienced member of staff doing the job you are interested in. Remember, though, that standards need to be expressed in *measurable* terms and should focus on *quantity* and *quality*.

The idea of EWS is important for training purposes and in the SHAPE system. The purpose of training is to enable an individual to meet the EWS requirements and, if the person is new to the job, to do so in the shortest time possible. As can be seen from Figure 2.6, a person who is trained will reach EWS much more quickly than a person who is not trained. It can only be achieved, though, if EWS is first identified and specified.

✓ **SPEEDTRAINING TIP**

Look at job descriptions and person specifications produced by your personnel department; they may contain specifications of EWS. If not, the information in them will help you determine EWS. It is quicker and easier to use personnel documents rather than starting from scratch.

Figure 2.6 *The idea of experienced worker standard (EWS)*

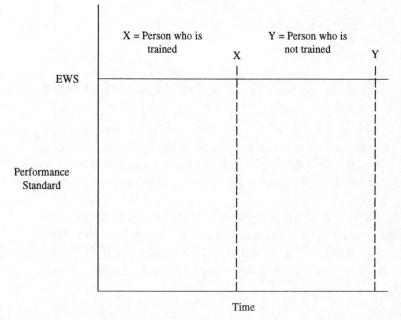

Personal Performance Requirement

Each member of your staff should be performing to the EWS for their particular job. From that point of view they are all the same, and all performing equally well.

It is not true, however, that every individual is the same: each is different and has different abilities and potential. To get the best out of each member of staff you also need to set and agree 'personal performance requirements'.

Personal performance requirements will vary between individuals, even those doing the same job. This element will focus on personal objectives which will be closely linked with the section and the team performance requirements; they will also be linked to individual abilities, potential and aspirations.

There are two well-established ways of setting and agreeing personal performance requirements:

- Staff appraisal
- Personal development plan.

The first is explained in detail in Chapter 4 and the second in Chapter 5.

Formulating Training Objectives

It should be clear by now that analysing and specifying performance requirements is essential to effective management. It should also be clear that training supports that effective management by enabling performance requirements to be met.

The way to ensure that this is the case is to utilize specifications of performance requirements to formulate training objectives. You may well be familiar with objectives for training activities somewhat similar to the following:

■ To introduce the new computer system

■ To explain and describe XYZ product

■ To examine the application of ABC policy

■ To develop the skills of interviewing.

The problem with objectives such as these is that they do not focus on *performance*. Effective management is performance-orientated; so too is effective training. Effective training therefore requires objectives which focus on performance.

Behavioural Objectives

Objectives are fundamental to training activity; they influence all other activities. To ensure a performance orientation you need to formulate training objectives in *behavioural* terms.

Behavioural training objectives have three components:

■ **Performance component.** This component specifies what the person will be able to *do* as a result of the training. It must therefore contain an action-orientated verb, eg:
  – Make
  – Operate
  – Construct
  – Repair
  – Complete
  – List.

■ **Condition component.** This component describes the conditions under which the person will be able to carry out the performance component. For instance, factors such as:
  – Using certain equipment
  – Using certain materials

45

    – Given certain information
    – Within a certain environment.

■ **Criterion component.** This component is the same as
  standards. It specifies the level of performance, ie,
  how well the person is expected to perform. As such,
  it focuses on factors such as:
    – Speed
    – Amount
    – Accuracy
    – Complaints.

There is a simple way to test whether a training objective
is written in behavioural terms – prefix the statement with
the phrase, 'The person will be able to'. If the statement
still makes sense then it is behavioural; if it does not make
sense it is not behavioural. Some examples of behavioural
training objectives are given in Figure 2.7 to further illustrate how they are written.

Figure 2.7 Examples of behavioural training objectives

1. **Typist** Produce letters and reports in company
   formant at a speed of 60 words per minute using
   ABC wordprocessing package on XYZ hardware.

2. **Assembly operator** Wrap and seal X items per
   hour using tape machine and staple gun and
   standard packaging materials.

3. **Sales assistant** Advise customers on full range of
   products in hosiery department within current
   stock range.

4. **Clerical assistant** Operate XYZ photocopying
   machine utilizing special features as necessary to
   meet requirements specified on printing requisi-
   tion forms.

Behavioural training objectives cannot be formulated unless performance requirements and standards are first specified. This is particularly true of the core performance requirements at the individual level. Having effective training objectives illustrates the importance of setting performance standards.

Summary and Checklists

The starting point of the SHAPE system is Setting performance standards; doing so is essential for effective management. All later stages of SHAPE assume performance standards are specified. Performance requirements and standards are needed at three levels:

- The section
- The team
- The individual.

Having performance specified at these three levels enables effective training objectives to be formulated in behavioural terms, and ensures that both management and training focus on what matters: *performance*. The following checklists summarize what you need to do to achieve that focus.

 SPEEDTRAINING TIP

Performance standards have to be known by those who have to meet them; so do your section's mission, KRAs and objectives so that staff understand the need for meeting their performance standards. Use regular and planned staff meetings to communicate this information. It is a waste of time to arrange special meetings.

CHECKLIST 2.1 – PERFORMANCE AT THE SECTION LEVEL

- Produce a mission statement

- Identify the key results areas (KRAs)

- Set and agree objectives

- Ensure objectives are SMART, ie:

  Specific
  Measurable
  Achievable
  Realistic
  Time-bound

- Specify standards

- Focus standards on *quantity* and *quality*

CHECKLIST 2.2 – PERFORMANCE AT THE TEAM LEVEL

- Identify the teams

- Determine KRAs for each team

- Set objectives for each team

- Set standards for each team

- Relate team performance to section performance

CHECKLIST 2.3 – PERFORMANCE AT THE INDIVIDUAL LEVEL

■ Identify core performance requirements for each task

■ Apply the idea of EWS to each job

■ Agree personal performance requirements

■ Utilize data to formulate training objectives

■ Ensure training objectives are behavioural and contain:

A performance component
A condition component
A criterion component

3 H: Harness Your Resources

3 H: Harness Your Resources

Introduction

We now come to the second element in the SHAPE system. 'H' stands for *harness* your resources. Harness is an appropriate word: it is normally associated with the tackle which is fitted to horses when they are used to pull a cart or carriage.

Why 'Harness'?

The two things that a harness enables a person to do with horses are also relevant to your resources. First, it enables the person to make the horses *do the work* for them; second, it enables the person to *control* the horses. Harnessing your resources through the SHAPE system has the same effects: you will make your resources work for you and you will control them to ensure that they do. But, like the person with the horse and carriage, you do have to *drive* and *steer* your resources.

Types of Resource

The first step is to know what your resources are. For the purposes of training your staff, they fall into five different types:

■ Time

■ Documents

■ Staff

■ Methods

■ Administration systems.

Two obvious resources are missing from that list. The first is money, or a training budget. Remember that the SHAPE system does not rely on external resources – SHAPE gives you the ability to manage the training of your staff yourself, whether or not you have a budget. If you have a budget, or access to a training department and training staff, then fine; add those to the list and use them. The SHAPE system, though, will ignore them.

✓ SPEEDTRAINING TIP

You may have a training department in your organization. If you have, invite them into your section to provide their services; they will be glad of the invitation. Specialist training staff can carry out a wide range of tasks, thus saving you time and effort. Remember though, *harness* this resource too. Get trainers to do the work for you but make sure you control them.

The second missing resource is you. You are in fact the most important resource of all. The way you put SHAPE into action will determine how well you use that resource.

We begin our examination of the five resources listed with the important category of *time*.

Time as a Resource

Time as a resource has three critical features:

- It is *finite*
- It *cannot be recalled*
- It is *equal*.

The first and last of these features are particularly revealing. Time cannot be added to or subtracted from; you cannot create more time. So, you have a fixed and finite amount available to you. The amount available is, though, the same for everyone. No person has any more or less time available than any other person – it just sometimes seems that way!

The second feature is also interesting. Think about your personal money as a resource. You may invest some in a building society account; later on you may decide to withdraw some to invest in some shares. You can therefore *recall* the resource. The same is not true of time: once it has been invested it has gone forever. Whatever return you get from each particular piece of time – an hour, a day, a week – is the most you can get for that particular investment.

Using Time Effectively

All of these features mean that time is a resource which must be used carefully. In order to make sure it works for you, you must:

- *plan* the use of your time

55

- *control* the use of your time
- *monitor* the use of your time
- *allocate* the use of your time.

This is not a book on time-management. What is important here is that you put those principles into practice in implementing the SHAPE system. In practice, you need to do the following:

- **Plan.** Decide *what* activities you are going to undertake to implement training for your staff and *when* each activity will be done. Prioritize time for training in relation to other demands.

- **Control.** Set *target* dates for completion of planning and preparation activities. Ensure other demands and activities *do not interfere* with training activities.

- **Monitor.** Review what you have *achieved* at regular intervals. Check *progress* against *target* dates. Revise your *plan* and *priorities* as and when necessary.

- **Allocate.** Set aside definite and regular *time slot*s for undertaking training activities. Make sure everyone knows what these slots are. Enter them in *advance* in your *diary* or other time management system.

 SPEEDTRAINING TIP

Utilize a time-planning/time-management system. Many are available commercially and very cheaply. They really work in practice and enable you to get the most out of your time in all areas of your job, including training. Those in common use, such as Filofax, achieve their popularity simply because of their effectiveness.

Figure 3.1 *Some tips on the efficient use of time in training*

■ **Utilize group training sessions for direct instruction whenever possible**
Training six people at the same time is obviously more time-efficient than training the same six people one at a time. Allocate the training to a time when all six are available. You can use any intervening time for other things.

■ **Deal with more than one subject in a session whenever possible**
Rather than have two or three separate sessions, combine related topics in the same session. For example, you may have decided to provide refresher training on customer-contact skills. You also know that in a short time a new product will be on line. Delay the customer contact training until the new product is available and combine them in the same session.

■ **Prepare thoroughly**
Sessions will run smoother, take less time and will not have to be repeated if you are properly prepared (see Chapter 5).

■ **Utilize other people**
Although you are responsible for training your staff, you do not have to do it all yourself. Use experienced staff members (see later in this chapter). Call in support staff from other departments, eg, personnel, accounts, administration. You can use the time freed up for other things.

■ **Use less-formal methods**
Training does not have to mean direct instruction. Many other less-formal methods are available which save your time – use them (see later in this chapter).

Getting the most out of the resource of time is simply a matter of effective time-management. *Harness* the resource: control it and make sure it works for you. Some tips on how to ensure efficient use of time in staff training are given in Figure 3.1.

Documents as a Resource

The remaining resources will all help you achieve the efficient use of time. This is particularly true of the second resource: documents.

Types of Documents

There are a number of documents which are required to provide effective staff training; they are all essential in the SHAPE system:

- Job descriptions
- Training plans
- Task analysis sheets
- Instructional plans
- Lesson plans
- Training specifications
- Administrative documents.

This may seem a long list. However, some of the documents are probably available to you from other departments; for instance, personnel will have job descriptions and the training department will have training specifications.

You will need to produce those documents that are not available. This will certainly be true of a training plan since this is *your* document to manage training activity in *your* section. Once the documents are available you will find them an invaluable resource. They will enable you to manage the training of your staff efficiently and effectively.

 SPEEDTRAINING TIP

Investigate the availability of documents in your organization's personnel and training departments. All it takes is a phone call – five minutes of your time to save you hours of work.

The Documents and SHAPE

The SHAPE system relies on you using these resources. How to produce the required documents is explained within the system. Chapter 4 deals with:

■ Training specifications

■ Task analysis sheets

■ Instructional plans.

Chapter 5 deals with:

■ Training plans

■ Lesson plans.

Administrative documents are described in a later section of this chapter.

The time you take to produce those documents that are not already available will be a sound investment. It will pay huge dividends since it is used to create an additional resource (ie, the documents) which has ongoing usefulness and value.

Staff as a Resource

It is not necessary, however, for you to produce every document yourself: you do have staff who work for you. They are, of course, your most important resource in achieving the required performance for your section. Your more experienced staff are in addition an important resource in managing and providing training and development.

Experienced Staff as a Training Resource

Experienced members of staff can be used for the following purposes in the SHAPE system:

- As a source of information
- To produce documents
  - training specifications
  - task analysis sheets
  - administrative documents
- To provide direct training
- To act as 'friendly colleagues' to new staff.

You do, however, need to *harness* this resource first. You cannot expect individuals to provide these contributions cold. The actions you need to take first are:

- **Select.** Experienced staff are not all equally willing and able to contribute effectively to staff training. You need first to think about who is most suitable from the point of view of being motivated and having appropriate skills.

- **Train.** Once you have decided which staff to involve, you need to develop their ability in appropriate areas. You can, of course, utilize SHAPE to achieve this. Pick the relevant elements of SHAPE, for instance assessing training needs at the task level from Chapter 4 for those producing task analysis sheets, and provide training yourself in the element to selected staff members.

■ **Compensate.** If involvement in training is not a direct responsibility of experienced staff, then they will probably require some recognition and reward. This does not always mean more money; more likely is the need to ensure that involvement does not mean *less* money. Where bonus or commission schemes operate, experienced staff may suffer if they spend time on training activities rather than doing the job itself. Their motivation will decline so you must ensure no monetary loss for involvement in training.

Delegating Training Tasks

 SPEEDTRAINING TIP

Delegate as much training activity as possible to supervisors and experienced staff. It saves *your* time; it also means less time overall is required. If it takes you one day, for example, to produce a training specification, using three or four staff means that four or five training specifications can be produced in the same time.

The more members of staff you can involve, the greater the resource you have available. The act of involving staff is also itself a training activity. Some experienced staff may aspire to managerial positions themselves. By enabling them to develop their ability in staff training you are in fact training them for promotion and, therefore, attending to their development. So, you have a double pay-off. Preparing your experienced staff for their involvement is also effective practice for you and an essential part of your development. There are, therefore, three good reasons for harnessing the resource of staff in implementing SHAPE:

■ Increase available resources

■ Provide development for staff members

■ Develop your ability in staff training.

CASE STUDY 2

Retail operations are notorious for high labour turnover. The problem is a serious one because success depends on high-quality customer service, which in turn depends on high-quality staff. High-quality staff can only be achieved by effective training. The effect of these two factors is that training cannot be ad hoc or left to chance.

All of this was well understood by Jane Laws when she became a branch manager in a regional chain of newsagents. Jane was determined to build the success of her branch on systematic and effective staff training.

Jane had been trained in the principles of the SHAPE system in a previous job. She quickly identified two senior and long-serving members of staff as a key resource. Working with these two individuals, Jane produced in a very short time all of the documents needed to implement SHAPE within her branch. The first training task Jane tackled herself was to train the same two people in all aspects of the SHAPE system. They were then given responsibility for organizing and providing training sessions for the rest of the staff, and for training new staff when they joined.

The effect of this action by Jane was dramatic. The training time for new staff is now less than half that previously spent. This is because all of the training is planned out and ready to deliver in the prepared documents, and because those giving the training know what they are doing. The two staff members chosen by Jane to be involved in training feel more valued and important. An added benefit, therefore, is their increased ability and motivation. Staff are proficient, customer service is high and Jane spends her time on other activities to further improve turnover and profitability of her branch.

Methods as a Resource

It is slightly unusual to view methods as a resource. They do though, properly used, do the work for you and enable you to control the outcomes. The greater the number of methods you are aware of and are able to use, the greater your resource base.

The Range of Methods

Methods in this context refer to providing training for your staff, that is, ways of developing the knowledge and skills of individuals who work for you. There are two broad categories of methods:

■ Formal, direct instruction methods
■ Informal, indirect instruction methods.

The first of these are the most commonly used and are described in detail in Chapter 5. Familiarity with the informal and indirect methods is the way to increase your resources. The following is a list of those informal methods which are essential to ensuring you maximize your resource base:

■ **Guided reading.** Often a member of staff simply needs to increase their knowledge on a particular topic; for example, a maintenance engineer in relation to a particular machine or a secretary in relation to the layout of formal reports. Providing guidance in terms of which technical or procedural manual or textbook to read is a simple, efficient and effective method of meeting the need.

■ **Delegation.** The critical element in delegation is that the task must be one which is your responsibility – you cannot delegate what is not yours. Giving a member of staff responsibility for a task you normally undertake is a very efficient and effective training method. Some common examples of tasks which are delegated for training purposes are:
 – Giving a presentation
 – Writing a report
 – Chairing a meeting
 – Handling a customer complaint
 – Planning work
 – Designing a new system or procedure
 – Selecting staff.

■ **Acting up.** Closely related to delegation is the method of 'acting up'. This simply means nominating a more junior member of staff to take on the role of a senior member of staff during a period of absence, eg, through holiday or illness. Such experience is extremely developmental for the nominated person. Doing the same for a senior member of staff during your absences is a form of extended delegation.

■ **Assignments.** This method involves giving an individual responsibility for a particular piece of work or project. The work must fall outside their normal duties. One common example of how this works in practice is to nominate someone for membership of an inter-departmental committee or working party. This not only increases their knowledge of the organization and the working of committees, it also develops their social skills and self-confidence.

■ **Visits.** Another method which increases knowledge, social skills and self-confidence is a visit. This is so simple, cheap and effective that it is surprising that it is used so little. Visits can be internal to other departments or external to suppliers or customers. An example of the former is where a member of staff processes invoices which are then paid by another department. A short, say half-day, visit by the staff member to that department can help to increase the efficiency of the whole operation. An example of a useful external visit is a maintenance engineer visiting the manufacturers of the equipment.

■ **Project/task groups.** This final method has the advantage of involving more than one person: it is a way of developing a group of staff. You simply form a project team from within your group of subordinates and give the team responsibility for a discrete piece of work. Common examples include planning the implementation of new products or equipment or procedures. One individual can be assigned a leadership role within the team, thus providing a further development opportunity.

Advantages of Informal Methods

All of these methods are simple, cheap (or free!), efficient and effective. They all provide an additional resource available to you in managing the training and development of your staff. One final method which lies somewhere between these informal methods and the formal, direct methods of instruction is coaching.

 SPEEDTRAINING TIP

One method not mentioned is job exchange. This is probably the most efficient and effective of all the informal methods. Simply put, it means two people do each other's jobs for a fixed period. The method costs nothing, is easy to organize and administer and results in training for two people at once. Use it whenever you can – it works.

Coaching

Coaching is one of the most effective methods for you to use to develop your staff. It simply involves utilizing the everyday experience of work and doing the job to maximize learning.

The obvious analogy is a sports coach. A team coach such as in hockey or football has a dual responsibility to each individual and the total team; so it is with you as a manager. In both cases – sports coach and manager – coaching involves the following:

■ Observing performance

■ Providing feedback

■ Identifying ways to improve performance

■ Agreeing objectives and targets.

The Nature of Coaching

A summary of what constitutes effective coaching and,

more importantly, what coaching is *not*, is given in Figure 3.2.

Figure 3.2 *Effective coaching*

Effective coaching involves:

- Viewing all work situations as potential learning opportunities.

- Controlled and planned delegation.

- Providing feedback on performance.

Coaching **is not and does not mean**

- Passing on your experience.

- Giving orders and allocating work.

- Inspecting work and TELLING staff how to do it better.

The aim of coaching is to help staff improve performance by developing their knowledge and skills, and you are more likely to achieve this aim if you adopt a certain approach to managing your staff. The required approach has the following features:

- A genuine interest in staff as individuals

- A demonstrated confidence in staff

- Being approachable

- Delegation of authority as well as responsibility

- An expectation of high standards of performance

- An expectation of finding potential in staff.

Coaching Styles

The approach also requires a 'reflective' style in dealing with problems and questions from staff. The range of possible styles adopted by managers is:

- Evaluative
- Interpretative
- Probing
- Supportive
- Reflective.

The first two styles are judgemental and have the effect of decreasing staff motivation. They share a second feature which is also true of the third style and that is that you, the manager, take responsibility for the problem. The effect of this is that staff learn dependence on you and also learn to avoid making decisions for themselves. This is the opposite of what you want from your staff. The first three styles are counter-productive in developing independent, innovative and confident individuals who are able to solve their own problems and make decisions.

The fourth style is more positive but again does not encourage development of ability and confidence. It is the reflective style which leaves responsibility with the individual, encourages thinking through and identification of solutions and develops ability. Figure 3.3 gives some examples of the reflective style in practice.

Coaching Skills

Coaching also requires the application of your managerial skills. The most important are:

- Listening
- Questioning

Figure 3.3 *Examples of a reflective response style*

Example One
A member of your staff has problems carrying out a particular task. You have called her aside to help her do it better. Your opening is something like:
   'How would you describe your difficulty?'

Example Two
You overhear a staff member dealing with a customer in an unsatisfactory manner. You call him into your office later in the day. You say something similar to the following:
   'You looked uneasy with that person. How did you see it?'

Example Three
One of your staff, in your judgement, has the wrong attitude towards a certain piece of work. You decide a chat may help to remedy the problem. You say:
   'How do you feel within yourself when you are doing this particular job?'

All of these situations are common. The approach illustrated by the reflective style responses focuses on the person and THEIR experience and feelings. This ensures responsibility rests and stays with them. In turn, this maintains motivation to change and produces developmental effects.

■ Observing

■ Analysing.

The sporting analogy of coaching also demonstrates an

important lesson of managing and training staff members. Once the 'players are on the field', they are on their own; you cannot do their work for them. This demonstrates the importance of effective training.

Administrative Systems as a Resource

The final resource you need to harness is that of administrative systems. As with method, this is often an overlooked resource. Getting the systems right, however, can make the difference between training being a smooth and efficient part of your section's operations or being an ad hoc and ineffective 'headache'.

Purposes of Administrative Systems

The most critical purposes of effective administrative systems, whether for training or other purposes, are:

- Planning
- Organizing
- Monitoring
- Controlling
- Coordinating
- Recording.

All of these are important management functions; they apply equally to managing the training of your staff as they do to any other part of your job. They also illustrate the importance of record-keeping. Training records can be of three main types:

- **Visual.** These are used for ready reference related to

present and future activities. Examples include planning boards, wall charts and diaries.

■ **Immediate reference.** These record information which may need to be referred to quickly at any time. Examples include card index systems and computer-held records.

■ **Long-term.** These records have long-term and ongoing value but do not necessarily require frequent or immediate reference. Examples include investigation reports and individuals' personal files.

Information to be Recorded

You will no doubt have these types of records for a variety of subjects. The kind of information you need to record for training is as follows:

■ **Personal details.** Information such as qualifications, training received, training planned, previous employments, length of service, appraisal reports, job changes, etc for each member of your staff.

■ **Department Activities.** This will include training plans, training programmes, numbers of staff trained in various tasks, etc.

■ **Reports.** Formal reports on training need to be recorded. These will include evaluation reports of specific internal and external training and annual reports on departmental activity.

■ **Reference information.** This final category includes that material you wish to refer to for training purposes. Examples include internal and external training brochures and perhaps this book!

Designing Record Forms

Many of these categories of information will require you to design your own forms for recording purposes. Below is a list of key points to apply to form design:

- Make them *brief*
- Make them *easy to read*
- Make them *easy to understand*
- Ensure they fit your *filing system*
- Ensure they conform to *company style*
- Ensure they are capable of use in a *typewriter*.

Before designing a form, it is important to:

- Define the *purpose*
- Define *who will complete them*
- Specify *who will use them*
- List the *information required*
- Consider *frequency of reference*.

Applying these simple guidelines will enable you to devise administrative and record systems which serve your purposes and which ensure the smooth running of training in your section. The following questions also need to be considered before finalizing decisions on your record system:

- Does it duplicate information readily available elsewhere in the organization?
- Can it be integrated into established systems, such as personnel or wages?

■ Is it capable of coping with future developments, eg, expansion of staff numbers?

■ How many people and which individuals will have access to which records?

■ Which information will be confidential and how will confidentiality be maintained?

■ Is the information really *essential*?

The final point is critical. Always remember that with any recorded information a golden rule is to *keep it up-to-date or don't keep it*. Figure 3.4 provides an example of a simple training record format.

Summary and Checklists

The 'H' in SHAPE stands for *harness* your resources. Resources available to you to support your training activities are:

■ Time

■ Documents

■ Staff

■ Methods

■ Administrative systems.

Harnessing your resources means controlling them and getting them to do much of the work for you. The following checklists summarize how to achieve that.

Figure 3.4 An example of a training record

Department: _____   Date appointed: _____

Name: _____   Date promoted: _____

Position: _____   New position: _____

Off the job training					On the job training			
College Courses	Qualifications Gained	Dates	Training Courses	Dates	Costs	Training Received	Dates	Objective	Results Achieved

CHECKLIST 3.1 – THE RESOURCES OF TIME, DOCUMENTS AND STAFF

■ Remember the three critical features of *time*:

> It is *finite*
> It *cannot be recalled*
> It is *equal*

■ Apply the four critical elements of time-management:

> *plan* the use of time
> *control* the use of time
> *monitor* the use of time
> *allocate* the use of time

■ Produce useful training documents

■ Include the following in your range of documents:

> Job descriptions
> Training plans
> Task analysis sheets
> Instructional plans
> Lesson plans
> Training specifications
> Administrative documents (see Checklist 3.3)

■ Utilize experienced staff in providing training

■ Apply their experience for the following purposes:

> Sources of information
> Producing training documents
> Providing direct training
> Acting as 'friendly colleagues'

■ Implement the following three steps in utilizing staff:

> Select
> Train
> Compensate

CHECKLIST 3.2 – THE RESOURCE OF METHODS

■ Utilize informal methods as well as direct training

■ Familiarize yourself with all available methods

■ Include the following in the methods you use:

> Guided reading
> Delegation
> Acting up
> Assignments
> Visits
> Project/task groups

■ Apply coaching as a sound development method

■ Carry out the following steps involved in effective coaching:

> Observe performance
> Provide feedback
> Identify ways to improve
> Agree objectives and targets

■ Apply the following managerial skills to your coaching activities:

> Listening
> Questioning
> Observing
> Analysing

■ Develop a *reflective* response style to your staff

■ Develop the following characteristics of effective coaches:

> An interest in staff
> Confidence in staff
> Being approachable
> Willingness to delegate authority
> Expectation of high standards
> Expectation of finding potential

CHECKLIST 3.3 – THE RESOURCE OF ADMINISTRATIVE SYSTEMS

■ Pay attention to developing effective record systems

■ Ensure systems aid the following functions:

> Planning
> Organizing
> Monitoring
> Controlling
> Coordinating

■ Utilize relevant types of record systems, including:

> Visual
> Immediate reference
> Long-term

■ Include the following categories of information in your system:

> Personal details

Department activities
Formal reports
Reference information

■ Check the following items before designing forms:

Define the purpose
Identify who will complete them
Specify who will use them
List the information required
Consider frequency of reference

■ Ensure your forms have the following features:

Brief
Easy to read
Easy to understand
Fit into filing system
Capable of use in a typewriter
Conform to company requirements

4 A: Assess Individuals and the Team

4 A: Assess Individuals and the Team

Introduction

The SHAPE system requires a thorough analysis of training needs; 'A' therefore stands for *assess* the needs. This has to be done at three related levels:

■ The team

■ The individual

■ The job and/or task.

The Importance of Assessing Needs

Identifying needs accurately is critical for successful training – you will waste time, effort and other resources if you do not do it right. The benefits of devoting enough time to assessing needs are tremendous: you will ensure all your staff have the correct knowledge and required skills to perform their jobs. This in turn will have positive effects on their willingness to apply their abilities and energies to achieve the highest standards of performance.

Training Needs Defined

What is a 'training need'? The best way to answer this question is to consider the diagram in Figure 4.1.

Figure 4.1 *The idea of a training need*

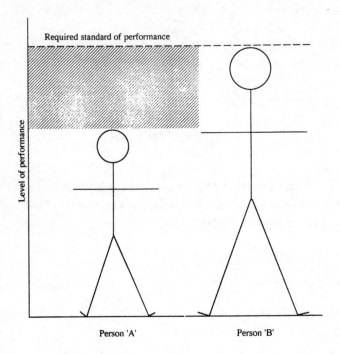

There are two individuals in the diagram, A and B. Person B performs a given job to the standard you require. The key reason why B does so is that B possesses the necessary knowledge and skills. Person A has some relevant knowledge and skills but they are not entirely the same as B. The existence of a difference between A and B means that A has a training need. The specification of that difference in terms of knowledge and skills is in fact a specification of the training needs of Person A. Person B is literally 'head and shoulders' above Person A simply because B possesses additional knowledge and skills. Once Person A possesses the same knowledge and skills, then A's performance will be equal.

Reasons for Performance Differences

There are many reasons for differences in performance between different individuals; some of the most common are:

- Personality
- Problems in personal life
- Dissatisfaction with pay
- Dislike of manager or colleagues
- Ability in performing tasks
- Familiarity with procedures.

The first two suggest mistakes in selection decisions. The wrong person is in the wrong job. The second two suggest problems in motivation: the person is not applying effort because of dissatisfaction at work. Only the final two examples indicate a training need, because they suggest a lack of skills or a lack of knowledge.

So, a training need exists where there is *a gap* between current knowledge and skills *possessed* by a person and the knowledge and skills *required* to perform a job. This idea of a gap is illustrated by the shaded area in Figure 4.1.

The Three Levels of Need

Our definition so far only defines a training need as an idea. To put the idea to practical use it has to be applied to the three levels at which training needs can exist – these are those listed in the introduction.

The Team

This level specifies the training needs of the total team. Needs at this level are of two types:

- Common needs
- Cumulative needs.

The second of these is simply a summary of all the training needs of all of the individuals in the team. The result is a statement, or *plan*, of the training required in your section in a given time period. How to draw up this plan is described in more detail in the next chapter.

The first type identifies needs which are held by all individuals in the team. Individuals do different jobs and carry out different tasks. They therefore will have differing individual needs. However, there will be some elements of knowledge and skills which are required in all jobs in your section. Such elements arise not because of particular jobs or tasks but because of the total work of the team; they are therefore common. One example is health and safety regulations and related methods of working. Others include the introduction of new administrative procedures such as for ordering supplies, or new computer systems to use in carrying out the work of the team.

The Individual

This level specifies the specific needs of particular individuals. The training needs of an individual are, as we have seen, the specific gaps in knowledge and skills that prevent the person performing satisfactorily. What the gap consists of is generally assessed by comparing knowledge and skills currently possessed with those specified as being required at the level of the job or task.

It is important to emphasize the difference between *training* and *non-training* causes of poor performance. You may be tempted to provide training for all staff to overcome all weaknesses. You will be wasting time and effort if the cause is not a training need. If the cause is related to low motivation or poor selection, then training will not improve performance. Training is only appropriate as a solution if the cause is lack of knowledge or skill. This is an example of why it is critical to *accurately* assess individual training needs.

The Job or Task

This level does not relate to a person. It is to do with a particular job or a specific task within a job. The idea of training needs at this level means specifying what knowledge and skills are *required* to perform satisfactorily.

It is not possible to assess individuals and establish their training needs unless the needs at this level have first been identified. The specification at this level provides the 'benchmark' against which a particular person's current knowledge and skills can be compared. The job- or task-level specification is equivalent to the knowledge and skills possessed by Person B in Figure 4.1.

Assessing Training Needs

There are different ways of assessing needs at each of these three levels. Each has to be carried out effectively in order to have a clear picture of the needs of your team and each individual member. How to do it is described in the rest of this chapter.

The Team Level

Needs at this level require an analysis of two separate factors:

- Performance
- Future changes.

Common Needs

Each of these has a different time focus. Analysis of performance focuses on current levels initially: you need to look at areas where improvement can be gained. A focus on future demands is also appropriate: you will no doubt be targeted to achieve improvements in performance in your section on an annual basis. Areas such as the following may be particularly important for you to consider:

- Sales turnover
- Unit sales
- Reduced costs
- Improved quality
- Reduced waste
- Increased customer satisfaction
- Labour turnover.

Highlighting areas for improvement in performance can indicate where training for the whole team will pay off. Similarly, changes being implemented in your section will create training needs for all or most team members. The time focus for this factor, though, is primarily the future. The question to ask is, 'What changes are planned over the next six or twelve months?' Some common examples of this factor are:

- Promotion of staff
- Transfers of staff
- New staff joining
- New policies
- New procedures
- New systems
- New machinery or equipment
- New legal requirements
- New products or services.

Considering the two factors of performance and future changes will enable you very easily to identify training needs which are common to the team.

✓ SPEEDTRAINING TIP

Keep your ear to the ground to anticipate future changes: read your organization's annual report; access and read important committee minutes and reports; keep in touch with managers in other departments and sections so you know their plans and how they might affect your section. Knowing in advance of future changes will enable you to plan ahead, identify training needs and be ready to implement the change when it comes. This saves time, money and effort.

Figure 4.2 *An example of a training audit form*

Name:	Age:	Length of Service:	
Job Title:		Section:	

Work Activities	Current Activity	Training Requirements	
		Refresher	Future

Cumulative Needs

You also need to have a clear picture of the total needs of the individual members of your team and a simple way of doing this is to complete a training audit for your section. An example format for doing this is shown in Figure 4.2.

The process of completing the training audit involves answering four questions:

■ **What are the activities?** First, you need to draw up a list of all the activities that take place in your section and enter them in column 1. This list must be comprehensive and complete. If you have separate groups of staff who undertake different kinds of work, eg, sales and administrative or production and maintenance, you will have a separate list for each group. Once you have compiled each list, you can continue to use it year on year. You will, however, need to revise and update your lists at least annually.

■ **Is X engaged in this activity?** Having compiled the list of activities you now complete a form for each member of staff. The first stage is to ask whether the individual is *currently* engaged in each activity in the list. If the answer is 'Yes', tick the box against the activity in Column 2. If the answer is 'No', leave the box blank.

■ **Is performance satisfactory?** The next stage is to consider whether the individual is performing to your required standard. For each activity you have ticked in the first column ask the question, 'Will X benefit from training to improve performance?' If the answer is 'Yes', then tick the refresher training column next to that activity (Column 3). If the answer is 'No', then leave columns 3 and 4 blank.

■ **Will X be required to do this?** The final stage is to consider each activity which is *blank* in Column 2. These are the activities which the individual is currently *not* engaged in. The question to ask is whether or not the individual will be required to undertake the activity in the future. If the answer is 'Yes', tick the future training column (Column 4). If the answer is 'No', leave columns 2, 3 and 4 blank.

The Value of a Training Audit

Completing a training audit form for each member of staff will enable you to identify the cumulative training needs of your complete team. When added to the common needs, you will have a clear picture of the total training requirements of your section. This picture will provide an essential piece of information for planning training, which is described in the next chapter.

The training audit is a simple and quick method of assessing training needs. In considering individuals' needs you will though also have to take account of the results of using the methods described in the next section of this chapter. To illustrate the training audit form and how to use it, an example of a completed form is given in Figure 4.3.

✓ **SPEEDTRAINING TIP**

Hold a half-day training meeting twice a year with a group of staff. Make the group representative of your department by having one person from each level and one person from each functional area. Discuss what training needs are likely to emerge over the next six months. This will help you to identify both common and cumulative needs for your section. It is a fast and efficient process.

Figure 4.3 *Example of a completed training audit form*

Name:	Steve Smith	Age: 33	Length of Service:	2 years
Job Title:	Senior Receptionist		Section:	Administration

Work Activities (Column 1)	Current Activity (Column 2)	Training Requirements	
		Refresher (Column 3)	Future (Column 4)
1) Greet and direct visitors	✓	✓	
2) Receive and sort incoming mail	✓		
3) Operate PABX system	✓		
4) Maintain visitor record book	✓		
5) Book visitors' car park spaces	✓		
6) Operate photocopying machine			
7) Select junior reception staff			✓
8) Training junior reception staff			✓
9) Etc			

The Individual Level

Going through the process of assessing needs at the level of the team will identify needs for particular individuals. This is clear from the following categorization of staff members:

- Newly appointed
- Newly promoted
- Those facing change
- Existing staff.

Training Needs of Different Categories

The first two categories will have obvious training needs associated with their personal changes: they need to develop the knowledge and skills required to perform their new jobs. The training needs of the third category will also be clear: they are the new knowledge and skills associated with the particular changes being faced in your section. All of these needs will emerge when assessing needs at the level of the team.

Existing staff will also have individual needs, some of which will be identified through the training audit. The process of asking the questions in the training audit is obviously one of *assessment*.

The focus of assessment at the level of the individual is *not* the person. Characteristics such as their likes or dislikes, interests, hobbies, age, beliefs and opinions are irrelevant for assessing training needs. The focus is on *job performance*.

Critical Questions

There are two critical questions in assessing an individual for training purposes:

■ Can the person perform the tasks required?

■ How well can the person perform the tasks?

These questions focus the assessment on performance. The second one also raises the important factor of *standards*: you need to assess whether the individual is carrying out their work to the required standard. The assessment will be against your standards, and these in turn will consist of specifications of the following factors:

■ Quantity

■ Quality

■ Method

■ Safety.

The final factor is important. Staff must meet safety standards – safety should not be compromised to meet, for example, quantity standards.

Any deficiencies in performance, either in ability to perform tasks or in meeting performance standards, will indicate the existence of a training need. You therefore need information about the performance of each member of staff.

Sources of Performance Information

There are three useful sources of information:

■ Performance records

■ Self-assessment

■ Appraisal.

Performance Records

The first source in the list will be readily available. It is part of your job as a manager to monitor the performance of your section and each member of your staff. You will therefore be able quite easily to establish for each individual whether they can perform the task and to the required standard.

Self-assessment

The second source is less commonly used but is very effective. The majority of individuals naturally assess their own performance. They too are remarkably objective. The individuals themselves, then, are a useful source of information on performance, especially if the information is related to assessing training needs. The next chapter describes the use of personal development plans, an approach which combines the activities of assessing individual needs and planning the training.

Appraisal

The final source is probably the most common method of assessing individual performance. You may operate an organization-based appraisal scheme, or your organization may not have one. Either way, it remains the case that you need to appraise each member of your staff as part of the process of identifying individual training needs.

Appraising Individuals

The word 'appraising' means almost the same as 'assessing'. The difference is that appraisal is more formalized and implies a face-to-face discussion between appraiser (you, the manager) and appraisee (each member of your staff). An appraisal process normally has the following features:

- A regular (usually annual) discussion
- Forms to be completed prior to and after the discussion
- Clear purpose and objectives
- A focus on future performance and improvement
- Aims to develop both motivation and ability
- Equal involvement of appraiser and appraisee.

CASE STUDY 3

James Stevens is a factory manager for a medium-sized garment manufacturer. His operation is one of three manufacturing units in the company and James carries responsibility for all aspects of business in his unit: finance, personnel, purchase and quality as well as manufacture.

The company has a very small corporate personnel department and does not have well-developed personnel systems. However, one service provided relates to management training. This comprises a series of short courses on management topics such as leadership, communication skills, use of information technology and budgetary control. The service also includes information on training courses provided by other organizations on topics relevant to garment manufacture. James used to find himself spending lots of time discussing and agreeing with his direct staff on who, if anyone, should attend which course. A major reason such decisions took up so much time was that there never seemed to be any consistent criteria or method for arriving at sound judgements, and the discussions cropped up at various points throughout the year.

To overcome this problem, James decided to design and implement a formal appraisal system throughout the factory. This enabled all managers and supervisors to identify the training needs of each member of their staff; it also enabled James to do the same for his senior managers. The system also ensured that discussion and decisions about training were focused on needs relevant to the business and that, in the majority of cases, discussions occurred at the same point in the year appropriate to the business planning cycle.

The effects of introducing an appraisal system were first, that the factory, each department and each member of staff had an agreed annual training plan; second, that James had to spend less time discussing and agreeing requests or suggestions for training; and third, that the whole senior management team was more confident that expenditure on training was accurately targeted to helping the business.

Successful Appraisal

Successful appraisal depends on a healthy and trusting relationship between manager and subordinate. This will ensure open and honest discussion of performance and identification of strengths and weaknesses. To achieve those conditions, the appraisal process needs to have the full support of those involved, including those being appraised. The following simple guidelines will help ensure that your staff support the process:

■ **Involvement.** Involve your staff in the process by inviting them to complete their own form prior to appraisal.

■ **Objectivity.** Do not use the appraisal meeting to

apportion blame or criticize individuals. Focus on strengths as well as weaknesses and give credit for achievements.

■ **Training.** Use the appraisal as a positive process to help your staff through accurate identification of training needs. Continue involvement here by encouraging staff to identify their needs themselves.

■ **Action.** Ensure that actions are mutually acceptable to you and the individual. Also, make sure that they are carried out and put into effect.

The use of preparatory forms by those being appraised is extremely effective in making the appraisal work. An example is provided in Figure 4.4.

Appraisal Meetings

The second most critical element is conducting the appraisal meeting. Such meetings are often referred to as appraisal interviews – this is too formal to set the right kind of climate; it also emphasizes the status differences between appraiser and appraisee, and who is 'in charge' of the process. Successful appraisal requires the support, commitment and full involvement of your staff. This is more likely to occur if they are in charge of their development. Referring to the discussion as a 'meeting' rather than an 'interview' will give the right message.

It is important that both parties are open and honest, and that the discussion is constructive. Achieve those conditions and you will have a successful meeting.

The primary time-frame of appraisal is the future and the main focus is identifying and meeting training needs. A record of agreed action to monitor implementation is therefore essential; an example is given in Figure 4.5.

Figure 4.4 *Example of an appraisal self-assessment form*

Name: Job Title:

Section: Date Completed:

1) List below your main activities/areas of work

2) What have been your main achievements over the last year?

3) Which parts of your job do you enjoy most and least, and why?

4) Which parts of your job do you find easiest and most difficult, and why?

5) What factors hinder you in performing your job?

6) Where do you think you could improve your performance, and how?

7) What training do you think would benefit you most over the next 12 months?

8) How do you see your career developing in the future?

9) What do you intend to achieve at work over the next 12 months?

The Job and Task Level

The third and final level at which training needs exist is the job and task level. Establishing needs at this level requires an analysis of the job and associated tasks in order to identify the required knowledge and skills.

Analysing Jobs and Tasks

The processes of analysing jobs and analysing tasks are very similar. The main difference is the level of detail included: a job analysis is very broad and is not carried out in great depth; a task analysis is more narrowly focused and goes into more depth.

Job Analysis

For many occupations a job analysis is sufficient to identify knowledge and skills requirements; examination of a job description can often be enough to produce a training specification. The training specification details what knowledge and skills are required to perform the job. As an example, part of a training specification for a receptionist is given in Figure 4.6. The process of arriving at the training specification is simply to take in turn each item of responsibility or duties which form the job description and ask the following questions:

Figure 4.5 Example of an appraisal record form

| Name: | | | Job Title: | | |
| Section: | | | Date of Interview: | | |

Agreed Training Need	Action to be taken by		Target Date for Completion	Review Date
	Appraiser	Appraisee	Training Department		

Signed: Appraiser _____ Date: _____

Appraisee _____

Figure 4.6 *Examples of a training specification*

JOB TITLE: RECEPTIONIST		
Job Description Item	Knowledge	Skills
1) Receive and direct telephone enquiries	1a) Operating of PABX system	1a) Finger dexterity
	1b) Functions of organization's departments	1b) Hand and eye coordination
	1c) Internal telephone directory	1c) Verbal communication

■ What does a person need to *know?*

■ What does a person need to *be able to do?*

■ What *attitude* is required?

The Use of Task Analysis

A task analysis is undertaken when more detailed information is needed, such as when jobs are more complex and/or safety is critical. A simple though clear definition of task analysis is:

> A systematic breakdown of activities required to carry out a specific task.

The process of carrying out a task analysis involves asking and answering three critical questions. The questions and method of answering them are as follows:

■ **What?**
  Break down the task into sub-tasks.
  Order sub-tasks into logical order.
  Identify any 'key points' in each sub-task, ie, points to emphasize.
  Check results of analysis.
  Record results in standard format.

■ **How?**
  Think through a familiar task at your desk.
  Observe an employee carrying out the task.
  Interview one or more experienced employees.
  Any combination of the above.

■ **Why?**
  To establish correct method.
  For assessing individuals' performance.
  To identify training needs of individuals.
  For use in providing staff training.

Carrying Out a Task Analysis

The above list constitutes a *task analysis* of *task analysis*. To analyse a task in your section you simply carry out one of the methods listed under 'How?' to establish the answers to the questions, 'What?', 'How?' and 'Why?' for that task. A simple format for a task analysis sheet is given in Figure 4.7. You can use this to structure your own analysis of tasks in your section and to record the results.

Figure 4.7 *Task analysis sheet format*

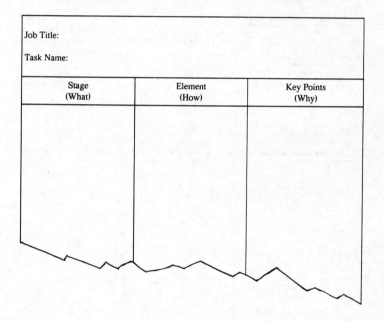

A part-completed task analysis sheet for wrapping a parcel is given in Figure 4.8 for illustration. The benefits of carrying out task analysis are worth the effort of doing so. The resulting specifications enable you to accurately assess whether a staff member performs the job correctly to the required method. They are also an invaluable aid in providing direct training to meet identified needs (see next chapter).

Once completed, task analysis sheets have continuing value.

Figure 4.8 *Example of a part-completed task analysis sheet*

Job Title:	Despatch Clerk	
Task Name:	Wrapping a parcel	

Stage (What)	Element (How)	Key Points (Why)
1) Pack item in protective box	a) Open box	a) Ensure correct quantity of packing straw
	b) Place packing straw in box	b) Take care in handling item
	c) Place item in box	c) Ensure box is secure
	d) Top up with packing straw	
	e) Seal box	
2) Wrap box in paper	a) Position paper on table	a) Portrait way for paper
	b) Position box on paper	b) Ensure edges are level
	c) Wrap sides	
Etc	Etc	Etc

Summary and Checklists

The 'A' in the SHAPE system stands for '*assess*'. You need to assess in order to identify training needs at three related levels:

■ The individual

■ The team

■ The job and task.

Establishing training needs accurately is essential for successful performance. The three levels of needs all require attention and effort. Below are three checklists which summarize the key points for each of the three levels. Put them into effect and you will have a clear and accurate assessment of training needs in your section.

CHECKLIST 4.1 – THE TEAM LEVEL

■ Assess recent section performance

■ Focus on:

> Sales
> Costs
> Output
> Quality
> Waste
> Customer satisfaction

■ Identify weaknesses and areas for improvement

■ Assess future changes

■ Focus on:

> Promotions/transfers of staff
> New staff appointments

Policies, procedures and systems
Machinery and equipment
Products and services
Legal requirements

- Identify knowledge and skills requirements

- Complete a training audit form for each individual

- Collate results of the training audit

CHECKLIST 4.2 – THE INDIVIDUAL LEVEL

- Categorize staff into one of four types:

Newly appointed
Newly promoted
Those facing change
Existing staff

- Access sources of information:

Individual training audit
Performance data
Self-assessment forms
Appraisal results

- Plan individual appraisals

- Ensure the following in the appraisal process:

Involvement
Objectivity
Training focus
Action orientation
Future time frame

■ Conduct appraisal meeting with each staff member

■ Adopt the six-stage approach to appraisal meetings:

> Preparation
> Opening
> Job factors
> Training needs
> Agreed action
> Ending

CHECKLIST 4.3 – THE JOB AND TASK LEVEL

■ Analyse job descriptions

■ Produce training specifications

■ Identify critical tasks in each job

■ Carry out task analysis for critical tasks

■ Use the following methods:

> Desk analysis
> Observation
> Interviewing experienced staff
> Any combination

■ Identify *what, how* and *why*

■ Complete a task analysis sheet for each task analysed.

5 P: Plan, Prepare and Present Training

5 P: Plan, Prepare and Present Training

Introduction

'P' in the SHAPE system stands for *plan* the programme; it also includes running the programme. In other words, this stage covers three activities:

- Planning the training
- Preparing the training
- Presenting the training.

Each of these activities has two separate contexts. The first is a plan and arrangements for its delivery for the whole section or department, the second is for each individual employee, or perhaps a group of employees with the same training need.

Planning the Training

The first activity requires application of certain key principles. These principles are best understood as a series of questions which need to be answered:

- Who is to be trained?
- How many require training?
- Where will the training take place?
- What broad methods will be used?
- When will the training take place?
- How long will the training last?

Answering these questions for each of your employees will allow you to produce a plan for your section. The overall plan will have a timescale attached to it: normally, this is one year, though you will need to monitor progress with the plan on a week-by-week or month-by-month basis.

Purpose

Having a written plan for the training of employees in your section serves a number of purposes; it:

- Identifies training requirements
- Provides objectives related to operational requirements
- Enables regular monitoring
- Communicates intentions to employees.

Each of these provides other benefits. For example, the last one will play an important part in motivating staff. All team members will be aware of what training is to be provided for the section. Each will also know what is planned for them individually.

Departmental Plans

A department training plan will record the answers to the questions given in the earlier list. Formats may vary. The important point is that *all* the questions are answered.

One format which is very simple but also very effective in use is given in Figure 5.1. The columns in the form should be completed as follows:

■ **Column 1.** List in this column the name of each employee in your section. If there are a number of employees with the same training need, simply enter their job title and the total number in the group.

■ **Column 2.** State here briefly the objectives of the training. The reason why the training is to be given often provides the objective.

■ **Column 3.** Indicate here the method of training to be used. Entries may include items such as direct instruction, reading, planned experience, etc.

■ **Column 4.** Estimate the number of days the training will take. Single training sessions can be counted as a half-day, so the entries in the column should be to the nearest half-day.

■ **Column 5.** This column enables you to allocate priorities between the various training activities identified in the plan. Allocation of priority at the planning stage will help if choices have to be made later on. One simple method of prioritizing is to use this code:
A = Essential
B = Desirable but not essential
C = Helpful if possible.

■ **Column 6.** Indicate here the date by which the training will need to have been completed.

■ **Column 7.** Identify in this column the person responsible for ensuring the training is carried out. In many cases this will be you as the manager, but sometimes it will be one of your experienced employees acting as an on-the-job instructor, or indeed the named individual to whom the training is allocated.

Figure 5.1 A department training plan

TRAINING PLAN

Department: _____ Period: _____
Manager: _____ From: _____
  To: _____

Name or Job Title	Objective of Training	Method to be Used	Number of Days	Priority Code	Target Completion Date	Action By
(1)	(2)	(3)	(4)	(5)	(6)	(7)

Figure 5.2 An example of a completed department training plan

TRAINING PLAN

Department: Accounts
Manager: M Smith
Period:
From: Jan 1992
To: Dec 1992

Name or Job Title (1)	Objective of Training (2)	Method to be Used (3)	Number of Days (4)	Priority Code (5)	Target Completion Date (6)	Action By (7)
All wages clerks	Able to use new computer system	a) Knowledge lesson b) Practical lessons	1 2	A	28/2/92	MS
B Kaur	Update knowledge on tax codes	Guided reading	1	A	31/3/92	BK
R Edwards	Able to operate photocopier	Practical lesson	0.5	B	30/1/92	BK
G Westwood	1) Able to complete all departmental returns	Knowledge lesson	2	B	30/4/92	MS
	2) Able to conduct selection interviews	a) Guided reading b) Practical lesson	1 2	C	30/6/92	GW MS

Training Plans as a Control Tool

Once this plan is completed you have a clear control tool to monitor training activity in your section. You can use it to check that required training has taken place and to check whether the training achieved the planned objectives. You can also use the time allocations and target dates shown in the plan for planning allocation of staff to the various operational activities of your section. Your departmental training plan will tell you who is not available because of training commitments and you will also know who will have what abilities by when.

To show what part of a completed plan will look like, an example is given in Figure 5.2.

Individual Plans

Plans for each individual member of staff are also very useful – they serve the same kind of purposes as the overall department training plan. Individual plans are usually called 'Personal Development Plans', or PDPs.

PDPs are produced for each individual. They will be one of the products of appraisal interviews. However, they need to be reviewed on a more regular basis than the annual appraisal process. The plans produced at annual appraisal will, though, provide the basic information needed to complete the annual department training plan.

Operating PDPs

To successfully operate PDPs the following points need to be put into effect:

■ **Regular discussion.** While the annual appraisal will produce a PDP, more regular monitoring and discussion of development needs is required. PDPs should be seen as flexible and as needs are met new ones may emerge. Discussion of PDPs should take place with each employee at least four times a year.

■ **Open communication.** There is, however, no need to have formal meetings for each discussion. The style should be informal and relaxed. Aim for open communication on progress with development. Give credit for achievements gained. Encourage the employee to reflect on and analyse their strengths and weaknesses. Be honest in your own assessment.

■ **Development focus.** Always remember that the focus of PDPs and the associated discussions is development. The focus should remain on training needs identified and met. Performance problems caused by other factors should not be raised in a personal development discussion.

■ **Performance- and career-related.** The purpose of PDPs is to maintain and improve performance, therefore discussions will require analysis of past, current and future performance requirements. Any identified improvements required should be achievable by additional training. Future career development can also be included in the discussions; training activities to help prepare for career development can be included in PDPs.

■ **Individual involvement.** A major benefit of PDPs is that individuals are committed to their own training. This will only be the case if they are firmly involved in devising PDPs. Individuals need to be encouraged to identify their own needs and to suggest ways in which they can be met.

■ **Shared responsibility.** Individual involvement needs to continue into implementation. Employees share responsibility with you as the manager for ensuring activities identified in the PDP are actioned. Their shared responsibility can be recognized by individuals being named in column 7 of the department training plan.

- **Range of methods.** Formal on-the-job training methods such as direct instruction are not the only ones to be used in PDPs. Personal reading or perhaps membership of project teams are two examples of less-formal methods that can be used. It is important to utilize the full range of methods available in PDPs.

- **Written plans.** As with department training plans, PDPs need to be written. Copies need to be provided to the individual employee as well as being retained by you. They will form the basis of the regular review discussions.

 SPEEDTRAINING TIP

PDPs spread responsibility for identifying training needs and devising ways of meeting them throughout the department. Every member of staff is involved in the process. This produces great savings in time and effort being applied by you and your supervisors. PDPs are not only effective, they are also efficient.

Format of PDPs

The format of PDPs needs to reflect the information requirements of effective training plans. For PDPs, the important items to record are:

- Person's name

- Date plan agreed

- Planned review date(s)

- Identified needs

Figure 5.3 *A personal development plan*

PERSONAL DEVELOPMENT PLAN

Name:

Department:

Date Originated:

Review Dates:

Development Items	Agreed Action	Target Date	Review Comments

Figure 5.4 An example of a completed personal development plan

PERSONAL DEVELOPMENT PLAN

Name: G Westwood   Date Originated: 2 Dec 1991

Department: Accounts   Review Dates: 3 May 1992

    3 July 1992

Development Items	Agreed Action	Target Date	Review Comments
1) Develop ability to deputize for Department Manager	a) Training on completing departmental returns	End April 1992	Training provided and successful. Will share work with M Smith in future.
	b) Training on conducting selection interviews	End June 1992	Training completed. Will sit as part of panel on next round of recruitment.
2) Improve ability and confidence in chairing meetings	a) Guided reading		
	b) Will chair final three monthly department meetings of 1992	End December 1992	

■ Agreed action items

■ Timescale for completion of each item

■ Comments/notes on review discussions.

A suggested format is given in Figure 5.3 and an example of a completed PDP is provided in Figure 5.4.

Preparing the Training

Department training plans identify the broad training activities to be carried out in a given time period; PDPs identify similar information for individuals. Where they meet is often in direct training provided by you, the manager. You therefore need to be able to design and prepare effective training sessions for your staff.

Basic Principles

There are some basic principles which underpin the design of direct training. These are to do with the learning process and the way people learn, and how this relates to giving instruction. The four most important principles are given below:

■ **Purpose.** The purpose of providing direct training is to transfer knowledge or ability to those being trained. You will have that knowledge or ability. Your training is only successful to the extent that your employees acquire the knowledge and/or develop the ability.

■ **The senses.** The five perceptual senses – sight, hearing, taste, smell and touch – provide the channels for transferring your knowledge or ability to your staff. They are the means used by learners to receive information from you, the instructor.

■ **Combining the senses.** New information is the basic

121

building block of learning. The more efficiently and effectively information is received, the more efficient and effective will be the learning. The more senses, therefore, that instruction methods utilize the better.

■ **Feedback.** Two-way feedback between instructor and learners is critical. Learners need to be told how they are doing against the standards expected of them. You need to know that your instruction has been understood. The use of questions by you is very important for both purposes, but words of encouragement and praise are equally important.

Principal Techniques

In applying these principles in practice it is possible to identify six major techniques of instruction. It is rare for any of the techniques to be used alone; however, mastery of each technique will enable you to select and prepare appropriate methods for your training sessions. The six techniques are:

■ **Telling.** A simple technique which is so obvious it often gets overlooked. Explaining and/or describing a given subject is an effective form of instruction.

■ **Illustration.** A technique which utilizes visual aids. Such aids do not have to be sophisticated: simple drawings on paper, photographs or, best of all, the object itself all constitute visual aids. Chalkboards or flipcharts, if available, together with films, videos and slides are the most common professional aids.

■ **Demonstration.** This technique means you perform the activity or task so that the correct method can be observed by your staff. It usually also involves the learners carrying out the activity.

■ **Questions and answers.** Again, an example of a simple and obvious technique which often gets overlooked.

Questions can take many forms and be used for different purposes. The technique will be described in detail in a later section.

■ **Discussion.** Here a group of learners elaborate and analyse the subject of the training. The discussion will normally be managed by you as the instructor.

■ **Supervised practice.** Your staff as learners obviously need to practise to build up their skill and develop their standards of performance in terms of quantity and quality. Standards being aimed for should of course be known by the learners. *Supervised* practice is important so that you can correct errors and provide feedback.

It will be obvious that these techniques utilize the senses in different proportions and different combinations. Those that utilize most, such as supervised practice, which can involve use of *all* the senses, are therefore generally most effective.

Principal Methods

Because of the need to use as many senses as possible it is normal to combine the techniques in any single piece of training. These combinations are referred to as 'instructional methods':

■ **The talk.** This method is used to provide background information. Such information is not normally essential to the performance of the task. A common example where the talk can be relevant is in induction training. The method combines the following techniques:
– Telling
– Illustration
– Question and Answer.

■ **The knowledge lesson.** This method is used to provide information which is essential to performing the task or activity. It is usually used with a group of learners though it can be used for an individual. It is also normally used prior to the practical lesson when dealing with skills training. The method combines the following techniques:
  - Telling
  - Illustration
  - Question and Answer
  - Discussion.

■ **The practical lesson.** This method is used to train in a practical ability or skill. It is the most useful to you as a manager in developing your staff. The method combines the following techniques:
  - Telling
  - Illustration
  - Question and answer
  - Demonstration
  - Supervised practice
  - Discussion.

■ **Group discussion.** This method is most relevant to training concerned with attitudes. Topics such as quality or customer service are common examples. You as manager lead the discussion to encourage the adoption of positive attitudes to the subject. The method combines the following techniques:
  - Telling
  - Discussion.

Figure 5.5 gives some examples of where you will use each of these methods and the purposes for which each can be used. The two you will use most often are the practical lesson and the knowledge lesson. How to deliver each of these is described in the next section.

SPEEDTRAINING TIP

Access whatever training materials are available from your training department. They may have standard knowledge lessons with standard aids, for example, for induction. Utilize your experienced staff and supervisors to produce standard knowledge and practical lessons. Share all the products around so that no one has to produce a lesson that already exists.

Presenting the Training

The major technique used in the practical lesson is demonstration. The following describes how to utilize the technique.

Demonstrations

Effective demonstrations depend on following a number of stages. These stages are in turn designed to apply a number of critical requirements:

- **Aim of demonstration.** The aim of a demonstration is to enable the learners to 'do it right' the first time they attempt the activity or task. Achieving this ensures that they do not pick up bad habits; it also ensures a successful outcome thus providing positive motivation.

- **Position of learners.** Learners should be positioned so that they can observe you carrying out the task. Rather than facing you, it is most effective if the individual or group of learners are placed to your side and/or behind you so that they see the activity from the *same perspective* as you.

125

Figure 5.5 *Direct training methods*

Method	Main Purpose	Example Applications
1) The Talk	To convey the same information to more than one person. Can incorporate questions from the learners and group discussions	a) Induction b) To inform staff of new policies c) To introduce new products d) To inform staff of department and organization performance
2) The Knowledge Lesson	To provide essential information to an individual or group of learners	a) Initial training for new staff b) For implementing new procedures c) Induction
3) The Practical Lesson	To develop ability in carrying out practical activities and tasks. Can be used for single individuals or groups	a) Initial training for new staff b) For implementing new systems c) For implementing new equipment
4) The Group Discussion	To encourage development of positive attitudes	a) Induction b) For implementing new policies c) To encourage efforts to improve performance

■ **Normal speed.** You should carry out the task at normal speed at least once in your demonstration. If you follow the natural tendency to slow down, you will achieve two negative effects. First, you will do the task differently and not how it should be done; second, learners will gain a wrong impression of what will be expected of them.

■ **Demonstrate silently.** Another natural tendency is to describe what you are doing as you do it. This also has two negative effects. First, your concentration on doing the task is distracted and therefore you change the way you do it; second, the learners' attention is drawn to your face if you are speaking and therefore they are not observing *what* you are doing and how you are doing it.

■ **Check understanding.** You need to check that your learners have followed and understood your demonstration. This must occur before they are allowed to try the task for themselves so that errors in understanding can be identified and corrected.

The Stages of a Demonstration

The most effective demonstrations take account of these requirements. One simple way of achieving this is to apply a clear, seven-stage demonstration method. The stages are as follows:

■ **Stage 1: introduction.** Introduce the session by stating the objective and describing the process.

■ **Stage 2: positioning.** Ensure the individual or group of learners can see clearly.

■ **Stage 3: first demonstration.** Carry out the task at normal speed and without speaking.

- **Stage 4: second demonstration.** Carry out the task with pauses to explain and emphasize key points.

- **Stage 5: third demonstration.** Carry out the task in stages with full explanation of each and re-emphasizing key points.

- **Stage 6: learner description.** Request the learner(s) to describe what you should do and how you should do it as you carry out the task for a fourth time. This stage enables you to check learner understanding.

- **Stage 7: learner attempt.** This final stage is for the learners to carry out the task. Observe them doing it so you can provide feedback and correct errors if necessary.

Applying the Stages

These stages taken together may seem excessive. However, they do have the effect of meeting the essential requirements. Most importantly, this method of giving a demonstration achieves the overall aim of learners *doing it right first time*. The method therefore is fully justified.

It is possible, of course, to amend the method. If the task is simple and/or if your staff are experienced and of high ability you can safely leave out one or two stages. Stage 4 is the least important in those circumstances.

CASE STUDY 4

Ashok is an accounts supervisor in the finance department of a local council. A major part of the work of his section is the processing of invoices from suppliers and the raising of cheques to settle them. Much of the work is routine and relies on the uniform application of well-established systems. There came a time, however, when complaints from suppliers about mistakes in payments and delays in settling accounts noticeably increased. This rise in complaints coincided with the introduction of a new piece of software to manage the payment system.

Ashok quickly realized that his staff were having problems with the new system. He had assumed they would adopt it quite easily; this was clearly not the case. Staff did not fully understand how the system operated. Ashok set about planning and preparing training sessions to overcome the problem. He gained help from a colleage in the computer section who had designed the system and involved a senior member of his own staff who would help with presenting the training sessions. Between them, they produced a knowledge lesson to be presented by Ashok and the computer specialist, and a practical lesson to be provided by Ashok and his senior staff member. Each would train half of the staff. The practical lesson made use of the demonstration method.

All three people involved in the training made use of common lesson plans and task analysis sheets. This ensured consistency in the training and in the performance standards reached by staff. The training itself was quick and easy to deliver. The effects were to reduce complaints and to raise the speed of processing invoices and thus the productivity of the section.

Knowledge Lessons

The knowledge lesson will be the second most common method you use to deliver training. Most often you will use it with a group of your staff, on occasions prior to providing a demonstration. The critical techniques used are telling and illustration. The telling component requires careful preparation to be successful. The following points need attention as part of your preparation:

- **Decide the scope.** You will need to decide the aim of the session; from that you can determine how much content to include.

- **Determine the order.** Once you have decided the content, you can then determine in what order to deal with the essential points. A useful tip is that people tend to remember best what they hear first and last.

- **Arrange the content.** One application of the previous point is the old adage, 'Tell them what you are going to tell them; tell them; tell them what you told them'. This translates into the following structure:
  - Introduction
    State the objective
    Outline the content
  - Development
    Cover the main items
    Follow a logical order
  - Conclusion
    Summarize the main points
    State the application.

- **Prepare notes.** Notes can be in many forms. If written in full remember that *spoken* speech is different from *written* speech. Write in spoken speech. It is advisable to write out the introduction and conclusion in full. Also, avoid difficult language, eg, jargon, slang, offensive words, words that are difficult for you to say.

■ **Prepare visual aids.** Remember drawings, photographs, models, brochures, etc can be just as effective as professional aids such as overhead projectors. If the subject is a physical object such as a machine or piece of equipment, for example a personal computer, then the object itself is always an effective visual aid.

■ **Formulate questions.** You will want to use questions in a knowledge lesson. It is best to formulate these and write them down in full in your notes as part of your preparation. This will ensure your questions are successful. It is more effective than trying to formulate questions in your head during the lesson.

■ **Rehearse aloud.** The old saying that practice makes perfect is not true; practice does, however, improve. Rehearsing aloud is the form of practice required for a knowledge lesson. It will also enable you to check your timings.

Presenting Knowledge Lessons

Thorough and careful preparation is critical to a successful knowledge lesson. It is like the bulk of the iceberg which remains hidden underwater but which supports the part which is visible. The visible part of your lesson also needs to be successful. Success depends on effective presentation skills. The factors listed below give guidance on what makes for effective presentations:

■ Voice   Be clear; no mumbling
Volume appropriate to size of audience
Speed controlled to avoid fast delivery
Vary strength and tone to avoid monotony

■ Personality   Be sincere
Smile and appear relaxed
Face the audience at all times
Engage eye contact, do not look at floor or ceiling

■ **Gestures**   Do not over-use
Avoid excessive body movement, ie, pacing or swaying sideways
Use open hands and arms
Avoid pointing with fingers

■ **Mannerisms**   Can become distracting
Avoid 'fiddling' with keys or notes, etc
Avoid verbal mannerisms such as 'Umm' or 'Er'
Natural mannerisms are not distracting if not excessive

■ **Nerves**   Feeling nervous is natural
Prepare well
Remember your feelings are not generally observed.

Lesson Plans

Whether you are delivering a practical or knowledge lesson, one result of your preparation will be some notes for your own use. Whatever form they take they constitute a lesson plan. Certain information always has to be included:

■ **The content.** Normally organized into main points and supporting points.

■ **The method.** Indicates the main method to be used by you at each point, eg, presentation, demonstration or discussion.

■ **The aids.** Identifies what aids will be used and when. A list of all aids required is also useful.

■ **The timings.** Shows how long is allocated to each part of the content as well as the overall session time. Can be based on 'clock time', eg, 2.00 – 2.15 pm and 2.15 – 3.00 pm, or 'actual time'; eg, 15 mins and 45 mins. The latter is more effective.

Figure 5.6 *An example of a lesson plan format*

<table>
<tr><td colspan="4" align="center">LESSON PLAN
Session Title: Duration:
Objectives: Aids required:</td></tr>
<tr><td align="center">Time</td><td align="center">Content</td><td align="center">Method</td><td align="center">Aids</td></tr>
<tr><td></td><td>Use main headings and sub-headings with supporting points; eg

1) INTRODUCTION

Objective:

Overview:

2) MAIN BODY

Include prepared questions in these notes</td><td></td><td></td></tr>
</table>

- **The questions.** Provides a written record of the formulated questions so they can be read off your notes.

- **The objective.** It is important to have this written out on your notes so it can be accurately referred to when required.

Layout of Lesson Plans

There is no one correct way to lay out this information. Some people use A4 notes while others prefer to use index cards. Figure 5.6 provides one common and very useful format for lesson plans. Use of coloured pens and/or highlighter pens is also very effective. Different items of information, eg, content, aids, questions, then stand out in your notes for easy reference.

Task analysis sheets are also a very useful addition to a lesson plan if you are giving a demonstration. In fact, a task analysis sheet can be the lesson plan for a demonstration.

✓ **SPEEDTRAINING TIP**

Prepare lesson plans for all sessions that you present on a regular basis. They can be used again and again and save preparation time whenever you deliver the session. Amend standard task analysis sheets for personal use as a lesson plan. Add in details of aids, questions and timings, etc. This will save you the bother of listing out the content separately.

Use of Questions

The final skill in providing direct instruction is the use of questions. You can use questions for three separate purposes:

■ **To check understanding.** You ask questions of your staff to check their understanding. It is most commonly used in the knowledge lesson but is also relevant in the practical lesson. The focus can be directly on knowledge covered in your instruction or can pose a problem not specifically included in the training but which cannot be tackled without the knowledge.

■ **To further learning.** You use this type of question to encourage your learners to think for themselves and to enable them to 'discover' the learning point for themselves. It is a useful question to use in discussions.

■ **To keep attention.** This purpose relates to when one learner allows their attention to wander from the lesson. You direct a question at that person to regain their attention. It is not possible, of course, to formulate questions for this purpose as part of your preparation.

Types of Question

Whatever the purpose, there are certain types of questions to avoid. These are:

■ **Closed questions.** These questions only require a one-word answer. That is not normally enough for the first two purposes. One particular form of the closed question is one which has only two possible answers, for example, 'Yes' or 'No'. That form is definitely to be avoided.

■ **Leading questions.** This form of question provides the answer required. For example 'Quality is very important, don't you agree?' That question is particularly poor since it mixes both a closed and a leading formulation.

■ **Multiple questions.** This form, as the name suggests, includes more than one question and often covers more than one topic. For example 'What do you think about the new quality programme and how will it affect our work and do you think we are up to it?'

■ **Tests of expression.** Questions which ask learners to describe in words some object or idea, test their powers of expression rather than their knowledge or understanding; for example, asking someone to describe the construction of a personal computer.

The type of questions to aim for are known as 'open questions'. These encourage and enable learners to give a full response. Such a response is a more effective measure of their knowledge and ability. Open questions generally commence with one of these words:

■ What

■ Where

■ When

■ How

■ Why.

Summary and Checklists

The 'P' in SHAPE encompasses *planning, preparing and presenting training*. All these activities need to be done well to get the most out of your staff. Below are three checklists which summarize the key points from this chapter. Used together, the checklists will enable you to effectively manage essential training activities in your department or section. Use them to assess your current performance and fill the gaps you identify.

CHECKLIST 5.1 – PLANNING THE TRAINING

■ Produce departmental training plans

■ Include information on:

> Objectives
> Who
> Where
> When
> Methods
> Duration
> Responsibility
> Priorities

■ Monitor the plan at least monthly

■ Agree personal development plans

■ Include information on:

> Staff member's name
> Identified needs
> Agreed action items
> Date PDP agreed
> Timescales for implementation
> Planned review dates
> Comments on review discussions

■ Hold regular PDP review discussions

■ Focus on the following in discussions:

> A development focus
> Open communication
> Progress and achievements
> Current and future needs
> Methods to meet needs

CHECKLIST 5.2 – PREPARING THE TRAINING

■ Utilize appropriate techniques:

> Telling
> Illustration
> Demonstration
> Question and answer
> Discussion
> Supervised practice

■ Combine into effective methods:

> Talk
> The knowledge lesson
> The practical lesson
> Group discussion

■ Apply the basic principles:

> 'Do it right first time'
> Use the senses
> Appeal to as many senses as possible
> Provide feedback
> Check and monitor progress

CHECKLIST 5.3 – PRESENTING THE TRAINING

■ Use the seven-stage demonstration method:

Stage 1:	introduce session
Stage 2:	position learners
Stage 3:	silent demonstration at normal speed
Stage 4:	demonstrate with emphasis on key points

Stage 5:   demonstrate with explanation
Stage 6:   get learners to give you instructions
Stage 7:   learners carry out task with your
supervision

■ Prepare knowledge lessons

■ Pay attention to the following:

Decide scope
Determine order
Arrange content
Prepare notes
Prepare visual aids
Formulate questions
Rehearse aloud

■ Practise presentation skills:

Voice
Personal presentation
Gestures
Mannerisms
Dealing with nerves

■ Use lesson plans with the following items:

The objectives
The content
The methods
The aids
The timings
The questions

■ Use questions for the following purposes:

> To check understanding
> To further learning
> To keep attention

■ Use open questions and avoid the following types:

> Closed questions
> Leading questions
> Multiple questions
> Tests of expression

■ Formulate questions using the following words:

> What
> Where
> When
> How
> Why

6 E: Evaluate the Results

6 E: Evaluate the Results

Introduction

We have now arrived at the final part of the SHAPE system. This final set of activities is concerned with *evaluation*. You need to check that your training has been successful and is giving you what you want; that is the purpose of evaluation.

Elements of Evaluation

There are a number of related elements that need to be monitored and assessed through evaluation:

- Acceptability
- Learning
- Ability
- Performance
- Results achieved.

These elements are connected. If the training is not an enjoyable and motivating experience your staff will not

143

learn. If they do not learn they will not improve their ability. If their ability does not improve they will not increase performance. If they do not increase performance the results achieved will not improve.

However, these connections are not simple cause and effect. Just because your staff enjoy their training it does not automatically mean that they have learned. Similarly, even if they learn it does not automatically mean that they improve their ability – and so on up to and including the results achieved.

This means that you need to monitor and assess each element separately to make sure each has happened, and that each has been successful. Where you identify problems you can take corrective action so that problems in one element do not have detrimental effects in another element. For example, if you find problems in *acceptability* you can solve them before they interfere with successful *learning*.

Factors to Evaluate

There are three factors which are common to evaluating the five elements but which vary in their application to each element:

- **Purpose.** The specific reasons for evaluating the element and the type of information you need to look for.

- **Methods.** The way you get information that allows you to check success or otherwise in each element.

- **Timing.** The point at which you apply the methods to evaluate the success of each element.

How each of these factors operates for each element is explained in the rest of this chapter.

Acceptability

It may seem strange to concern yourself with the acceptability of training to your staff. However, individuals' experience of particular and specific training sessions will affect their success. Staff are also a source of good ideas on how to improve training sessions.

Purpose

There are two broad purposes to evaluating the element of acceptability: to check staff experience of training sessions and to gain their ideas on improving training. Specifically, the purposes are:

■ To check the level of enjoyment and motivation

■ To check whether the training was seen as relevant

■ To check whether the delivery was acceptable

■ To gain ideas from staff on how to improve training.

The list of purposes suggest a number of areas you need to focus on in this element. The most important are:

■ **Content.** Questions such as was there too much or too little and was it too complicated or too simple need to be asked.

■ **Methods.** Here opinions on the mix and balance of methods is required. For example, in a knowledge lesson staff may have preferred more time for questions.

■ **Trainer style.** This area is to do with staff reaction to the person who delivers the training. That person may of course be you! It is, though, important to gain comments on how the trainer deals with staff, eg, helpful/unhelpful, clear/unclear communicator, etc.

- **Duration.** The final area is the length of time taken to do the training, eg, too long and spread out or too short and intense.

It can also be useful to gain information on topics which are seen as important by particular individuals. This is best achieved by having an 'open' rather than focused area of questions.

Methods

There are two main methods of gaining the information you require in this element:

- Verbal
- Written.

The first simply involves holding a discussion with the individual or group of staff being trained. You focus the discussion by asking questions about the different areas.

The written method means designing a questionnaire and asking staff to complete it. The questionnaire should ideally be short and simple. A typical example is shown in Figure 6.1.

✓ **SPEEDTRAINING TIP**

Check whether your training department has a standard form they use to evaluate the element of acceptability. Perhaps a colleague manager has devised one, or you may have one from a course you attended. Any of these will be a source of ideas and so save you time in designing your own.

Figure 6.1 *Acceptability element – example of a questionnaire*

Session Title: Date(s):
Name: Position:

1. Content
   a) What do you think about the content of the training session?

   b) Which additional topics, if any, should have been included?

   c) Which topics, if any, could have been omitted?

2. Methods
   a) What do you think about the methods used in the training session?

   b) Which methods, if any, would you have liked to be used *less* often?

   c) Which methods, if any, would you have liked to be used *more* often?

3. The Trainer
   a) Please give your comments about the Trainer.

4. Duration
   a) Was the training session too long or too short or about right? Please give reasons for your answer.

5. Other Comments
   a) Do you have any other comments on how to improve the training session?

There is in fact a third method which is more informal: *observation*. Acceptability concerns the response of staff to training. Their responses can be fairly easily monitored by simply observing their behaviour as the training happens.

Timing

The informal method of observation can and should be applied continuously. Timing, therefore, for acceptability is at regular points throughout the training activity.

The formal methods of verbal and written responses are usually applied immediately at the end of a training activity. This does not, however, necessarily mean at the end of the *total* activity. Most training sessions consist of separate parts. For example, in a knowledge lesson you may give a talk followed by a question and answer session followed by a group discussion. Each of these separate parts can be assessed independently as well as the total lesson.

Learning

This element is the first where more objective assessment is possible. Acceptability focuses on the personal responses of individuals. The learning element is more open to objective measures of success.

Purpose

The primary purpose of this element is to assess the extent of learning achieved by the training activity. Specifically, the purposes are:

■ To assess what staff *know* at the end of training

■ To assess what *skills* have been acquired or improved

■ To check whether the *objectives* of the training have been achieved.

Methods

These separate purposes indicate that a range of different methods need to be applied in this element depending on the nature of the training objectives. For instance, objectives which relate to *knowledge* will require different methods from objectives which relate to *skill.*

Essentially, evaluating the learning element requires *testing* staff at the end of training activities. Such tests can take a variety of forms:

■ **Knowledge tests.** Quizzes, true/false statements, short answer questions, multiple-choice questions and completion statements are all different forms of knowledge tests. These examples are usually based on written tests rather like examinations for qualifications. You can also test knowledge through verbal questioning.

■ **Skills tests.** Work samples, simulated test pieces, case studies, role plays and exercises are examples of methods for assessing skills. The focus of skills tests is on what staff *can do* as opposed to what they *know.*

Some examples of both knowledge tests and skills tests are given in Figure 6.2. The examples are based on the behavioural training objectives in Figure 2.7 in Chapter 2.

The actual methods you can use to collect information and apply the tests to assess learning fall into four broad categories:

■ Written

■ Verbal

Figure 6.2 *Learning element – examples of tests*

1. **Sales Assistant – knowledge on tights**
   a) List below *all* brands of tights stocked in the hosiery department.

   b) Give at least *four* reasons for differences in price between different brands.

   c) How would you determine the size of tights required by a particular customer?

   d) Which of the following features are *true* of ABC brand?

	True	False
All sizes available		
15 colours and shades		
Firm support available		
Only available in 15 denier		
Contains Lycra		
Machine washable		

2. **Clerical Assistant – Skills test**
   Produce 25 stapled copies of five-page test original reduced to A5 size.

■ Practical

■ Observation.

Knowledge tests usually utilize Written or Verbal while Skills Tests normally use Practical and Observation. Many people avoid tests to assess learning because they are uncomfortable with their use and therefore rely solely on Observation. There is though only one way to be sure of the extent of learning achieved by training and that is by testing.

 SPEEDTRAINING TIP

Devise standard tests you can use for training that is done regularly; use supervisors and experienced staff in completing this task. Both actions save you time and make the task easier.

Timing

As with the acceptability element, learning is usually assessed at the end of training, but it can also be monitored and assessed within the training activity. This provides two broad categories of tests which are applied at different points:

■ **Phase tests.** These are tests which are used at the end of particular parts of training to check and monitor progress. For example, a receptionist needs to know who does what in each department or section. The individual can be tested on knowledge of department A before moving on to learn about department B and

151

then be tested on B before moving on to learn about department C.

- ■ **End tests.** As the name implies, end tests are used at the end of the total training activity. In the example of the receptionist, the end test would assess knowledge of all departments.

Precise timing will vary according to the nature and length of particular training activities. End tests, though, need to be almost immediate. So, for example, in a piece of training which lasts a day, the final 30–60 minutes would be used for assessing learning. If problems are identified, eg, learning is not complete, corrective action can be planned and taken.

Ability

Once your staff have learned, they should have the ability to carry out the tasks required of them in their jobs. This is the next element to be evaluated.

Purpose

The primary purpose of evaluating at this level is to check that the training was relevant. Staff may have learned successfully but they may have learned the wrong things. The specific purposes in this element are, therefore:

- ■ To check the relevance of learning achieved
- ■ To assess improvement in ability
- ■ To check ability in the job.

Methods

This element requires individuals to actually carry out

tasks associated with their job in the work place and under normal work conditions. The carrying out of the tasks will normally be supervised by you or the staff member's supervisor for evaluation purposes.

There are three methods used to collect information in this element:

- **Observation.** This method simply means watching the individual carry out the task. It provides another opportunity for corrective action if required.

- **Supervisors' reports.** You request a report from supervisors to check on ability of individuals. If they carry out the observation, this method can also be combined with and focus on the third method.

- **Work output.** This method requires an analysis of the work of the individual, focusing on the output achieved, eg, how much is typed by a typist or how much is sold by a sales assistant. Monitoring of work output and the subsequent analysis can be carried out by supervisors.

Timing

Since this element focuses on ability to do the job, it cannot be applied during the training. The timing of this element therefore is after the completion of the total training activity.

Actual timing will vary from job to job. As a general guide, it should be within one month of the training. For some jobs, though, it may be as little as two or three days following the completion of training. Again as a general guide, the simpler the job, the less time is required after training to evaluate the element of ability.

CASE STUDY 5

Kim is a quality control engineer in a small engineering firm. She is responsible for ensuring that finished goods, usually in the form of component parts for assembly into automotive products, meet customer specifications. Kim has responsibility for five staff who are all professionally trained.

The members of Kim's work team are tightly knit and meet regularly. Because of the increasing interest in and availability of new techniques for quality control, Kim and her staff have been receiving significant amounts of training. There have been increasing signs of resentment from other managers and staff in the company about this and Kim herself became concerned that the training was not of real value. She also wanted to protect her staff from unfair accusations of special treatment.

An obvious answer to this problem was to apply some of the principles of quality control to training activity. Kim designed and applied a comprehensive evaluation system. This enabled her to be satisfied about the various training courses and providers she and her staff had been using. As a result, some of the courses and providers were no longer used. Kim found also that she was in a position to justify and demonstrate the benefits of the training she and her staff were receiving.

An added bonus of this experience was that the evaluation system used in the quality control department was adopted throughout the company. All of Kim's colleague managers are satisfied that they too can now effectively evaluate their training investment.

Performance

Once individuals have the required ability they should be producing the required performance within a short time-scale. It is, however, unrealistic to expect full performance immediately – individuals need practice and experience in the job to sharpen their skills and to build their confidence.

Purpose

The purpose of this element of evaluation is to assess actual performance achieved. The detailed purposes are:

■ To check performance levels

■ To assess performance standards achieved against EWS

■ To ensure training pays off in terms of individual performance.

Methods

The methods used to evaluate this element are a repeat of the previous element. In addition, you can also use performance appraisal. This is particularly relevant when training has been provided to enable an individual to achieve personal performance requirements or personal objectives (see Chapter 2). Appraising the level of achievement of personal objectives provides an assessment of the success of the training in terms of the performance element.

In summary, there are four methods in this element:

■ Observation

■ Supervisors' reports

■ Analysis of work output

■ Performance appraisal.

Timing

Since reaching performance at EWS level requires time and experience of doing the job, this element of evaluation cannot be applied until a while after completion of training. It also has to occur after the ability element has been evaluated.

Actual timing will again vary from job to job. A maximum period for the vast majority of jobs is three months. The time will be much less for many jobs; perhaps as little as one week for very simple, low-level tasks. The general guide that the simpler the job the less time required, also applies to the performance element of evaluation.

 SPEEDTRAINING TIP

Use supervisors to evaluate performance. They can monitor and assess work output, which will form the basis of their reports to you. It spreads the load and makes the task more efficient.

Results Achieved

The final element is the most important. Success or otherwise here determines whether training has been worthwhile and whether you receive any return for your investment of time and effort.

If other elements indicate success, it is also likely in this final element. If your staff are all performing at EWS or better and achieving their personal objectives then there will be obvious benefits for your section.

Purpose

The main purpose of this element focuses on the effects of training on the overall performance of your section. Specifically, they are:

■ To check the overall results of training activities

■ To assess the benefits to the section

■ To determine whether investment in training has been worthwhile.

Methods

The methods used in evaluating the results achieved are those that you use to monitor and review the overall performance of your section. They are likely, therefore, to include:

■ Weekly and monthly performance figures

■ Monthly and annual returns

■ Annual reports

■ Your personal appraisal with your manager.

The focus of most of these measures will be the mission, KRAs and objectives for your section (see Chapter 2). The degree of success you achieve in meeting these performance requirements for your section is the ultimate measure of success for your training activities.

In applying these measures, you have to allow for other factors which influence achievement. Not all success can be attributed to training; similarly, not all failure is caused by poor training. What is certain is that success is probably impossible without sound training.

Timing

Final results achieved by training obviously take time to work through and demonstrate themselves in measurable outcomes. Also, since the focus and methods in the results achieved element are the normal performance monitoring procedures used in your section, you will find it more efficient to combine evaluation with those procedures.

For these two reasons, evaluating training in the results achieved element should be a minimum of three months after completion of the training activity. In some cases, for instance if you recruit a significant number of new staff at the same time, this final element of evaluation will not be applied until six months after completion of training. So, timing in this element will be between a minimum of three and a maximum of six months.

Summary and Checklists

Evaluating training serves the dual purposes of checking results achieved and demonstrating the benefits. It is the final set of activities within the SHAPE system. Applying the activities involved in evaluation will help you ensure you achieve the results you want from investing time and effort in managing the training of your staff.

Evaluation has to be applied within the following five elements:

- Acceptability
- Learning
- Ability
- Performance
- Results achieved.

Each element varies in its *purpose* and *methods* used and

in the *timing* and application. The following checklists summarize these factors for each element.

CHECKLIST 6.1 – THE ELEMENT OF ACCEPTABILITY

■ Purpose
To check the level of enjoyment and motivation
To gain ideas to improve training

■ Methods
Verbal questioning and group discussions
Written questionnaires
Each of the above to focus on:
Content
Methods
Trainer style
Duration

■ Timing
Continuous throughout training
Immediately on completion of training

CHECKLIST 6.2 – THE ELEMENT OF LEARNING

■ Purpose
To check the acquisition of knowledge and skills
To check achievement of training objectives

■ Methods
Knowledge and skills tests which can be:
Written
Verbal
Practical
Observation-based

- Timing
  Immediately after completion of training

CHECKLIST 6.3 – THE ELEMENT OF ABILITY

- Purpose
  To assess improvement in ability
  To check ability to do the job

- Methods
  Observation
  Supervisors' reports
  Work output

- Timing
  Within *one month* following completion of training

CHECKLIST 6.4 – THE ELEMENT OF PERFORMANCE

- Purpose
  To assess performance against EWS
  To ensure training is successful for individuals

- Methods
  Observation
  Supervisors' reports
  Work output
  Performance appraisal

- Timing
  Within *three months* following completion of training

CHECKLIST 6.5 – THE ELEMENT OF RESULTS ACHIEVED

■ Purpose
To check overall results of training
To assess the benefits in relation to the investment of time and effort

■ Methods
Monitoring of section performance
Regular performance reports
Performance appraisal

■ Timing
Within *six months* following completion of training

7 Reaping the Rewards of SHAPE

7 Reaping the Rewards of SHAPE

Introduction

You will be glad to know that this final chapter is very short. However, it is also the most important in the book, because it provides the final advice on how to get the best out of your staff through implementing SHAPE.

The Benefits of SHAPE

As a reminder, the potential benefits of SHAPE were identified in Chapter 1 as:

■ Reduced waste of materials

■ Reduced errors and re-work

■ Reduced learning times

■ Increased quality

■ Increased flexibility

■ Increased individual performance

■ Reduced accidents

■ Reduced absenteeism

- Reduced labour turnover

- Reduced complaints.

These are impressive benefits and well worth achieving. They will have direct and measurable effects on the performance of your section.

SHAPE and Speedtraining

Remember too that the main benefit of SHAPE is its effect of speeding up the training process. This in itself brings additional benefits:

- Saves your time as a manager

- Allows you to devote attention to other activities

- Enables you to respond to change speedily and effectively

- Provides a competitive advantage

- Builds training into the everyday work of your operation

Coping with rapid and continuous change is the biggest challenge facing managers of organizations today. All the predictions for the future agree that this situation will not alter; it will only become more and more true. Success will increasingly depend on your ability to manage and implement change. Speedtraining through SHAPE will provide you with a critically important method of doing just that. (Further consideration of the role of training in the management of change can be found in Appendix 2 on page 179.)

So, the question that now arises is how you can make sure you achieve all these potential benefits.

Achieving the Benefits of SHAPE

There is only one way to gain the benefits of SHAPE – use it. This in turn requires you do two things:

■ Implement SHAPE

■ Incorporate SHAPE into your management practice.

These are not the same. You could implement SHAPE as a special project this year and then never use it again. If you do you will not gain all the benefits and those you do gain will not last. You must therefore *continuously* implement SHAPE by making it part of the way you manage.

In order to incorporate SHAPE into your management practice you need to carry out five steps:

■ **Know the system.** You cannot implement SHAPE successfully and continuously unless you are fully familiar with what it involves. Make sure you are familiar by reading and re-reading chapters in this book. Keep the book available for reference.

■ **Assess personal practice.** Once you are familiar with SHAPE you need to compare what you do now with what is suggested in the system. It is probable that you already do some of the things advised in SHAPE. You do, though, need to identify those activities in SHAPE which are lacking in your current practice.

■ **Assess the organization's practice.** A similar exercise is required for your organization. Does it have a training department? Does that department produce skills analysis sheets and training specifications? They may use different names but any services or documents available to you from central personnel or training departments will help and affect how you implement SHAPE.

■ **Select checklists.** The checklists at the end of each chapter summarize the key points. They can be used for both familiarizing the content and for quick and easy reference. Use your personal and organization assessment to identify which checklists are most relevant to improving your management practice.

■ **Be systematic.** The SHAPE system is a systematic approach to training and development. The five sets of activities in the system are intended to be sequential. Start with S and carry out those activities you need to up to and finishing with E.

Once you have carried out these steps you will be in a position to incorporate SHAPE into your management practice. Simply put all the SHAPE activities into effect in the correct order on a regular basis.

Getting Started

The first actions you take to implement SHAPE will be critical. If you do not find them easy, or if you do not begin to see the potential benefits, you may well be inclined to give up.

One way of ensuring you do not encounter these problems is to spend some time first *planning* your actions. This entails writing out an action plan. Producing an action plan is the best way of getting started.

Figure 7.1 contains a suggested format. The headings are explained below:

■ **Item.** List in this column the action items you intend to undertake. Examples might include the five steps listed earlier, or you might want to be less ambitious at first and therefore limit your action plan to the first step.

Figure 7.1 *Action plan format*

Item	Objective	Method	Target

- **Objective.** Identify here what you intend to achieve by each action item. It is best to think about objectives in terms of changed conditions. For example, instead of writing 'To produce training plan' express the objective as 'Training plan completed'.

- **Method.** Against each item and following the objective, this column is used to identify the specific steps you will take to achieve the obective. You are likely to have three or four entries for each action item. For instance, if the item is to do with setting standards your methods may look something like this:

- Arrange meeting with work study department (WSD)
- Review standards set by WSD with supervisors and experienced staff
- Meet with manager to discuss and agree standards
- Produce and distribute statements of standards.

■ **Target.** The final column relates to timescale. Set a date for completion of each action item. Check achievement of the objective on this date and revise your action plan if required.

Consciously thinking about how you are going to use SHAPE and planning ahead will make it more likely that you actually put it into practice – and then you will reap the benefits.

Conclusion

The SHAPE system will not manage for you; it is not a universal solution to all your problems as a manager. It is, though, an effective way of taking charge of a critical part of your job. SHAPE enables you to control the training of your staff and therefore to maximize their performance.

The future for all organizations, including yours, is uncertain. Success and prosperity can only be achieved by an able and motivated workforce. Ability and motivation are both dependent upon effective training. Your success and that of your organization requires more attention to training in the future than has been the case in the past. Take charge of the future. SHAPE it to your vision.

Appendix 1:
Index of Speedtraining Tips

Appendix 1:
Index of Speedtraining Tips

This index highlights six critical themes of managing and training staff, and summarises the **Speedtraining Tips** provided in the text which relate to each theme.

Communication

Communicating is a critical activity for managers. The relevant tips are listed in the order they appear in the text with the page beside.

(p 47)   Use regular and planned staff meetings to communicate performance standards and objectives.

(p 87)   Make sure you maintain a wide network of contacts and keep in regular communication with them. In this way you will know in advance about future changes and how they might affect your section.

(p 90)   Hold a half-day training meeting twice a year with key staff to discuss likely training needs over next six months.

(p 99)   Proper preparation is crucial in getting the most out of the communication opportunity that occurs through appraisal.

(p 118) Personal development plans are both effective and efficient as a way of ensuring regular, face-to-face communication between manager and staff.

Resources

Resources, and getting the best out of them, are extremely important in a manager's job. The following tips offer practical advice.

(p 54) Get the best out of your training department by inviting specialist staff into the line department. It is a *resource* paid for by all line or operational departments so make sure you harness it.

(p 59) Documents are a resource which often save time. Investigate their availability in your organization's personnel or training department to save you the effort of 're-inventing the wheel'.

(p 61) Delegate as much training activity as possible to supervisors and experienced staff. It saves *your* time.

(p 66) One training method that saves you both time and money is arranging a job exchange between two people.

(p 156) Use supervisors to evaluate performance. They can monitor and assess work output, which will form the basis of their reports to you. It spreads the load and makes the task more efficient.

Specifications

Managers need to create and apply specifications – of standards, of performance, of work methods, etc. The tips listed below refer to creating and/or using specifications for training purposes.

(p 38)   Use available information, for instance bonus or commission schemes, to specify standards. This will save you the time and effort needed to produce specifications.

(p 43)   Use additional specifications available from personnel departments. Job descriptions may help you determine experienced worker standards without starting from scratch.

(p 125)   Use examples of materials that may be available from training departments in the form of specified instruction plans to ensure that no one spends time reproducing an existing lesson plan. Also use experienced supervisors to produce similar standard lessons.

(p 151)   Devise standard specifications or tests for use in the final stages of a training evaluation process that is done regularly.

Systems

As with specifications, managers also have to create and apply systems. The purpose of systems is to make life easier. The following list of tips suggests some ways of achieving that in relation to training and development.

(p 56)   Use time-management/time-planning systems to help you get the most out of your time.

(p 99)   Remember that it is not the system itself which is important, but how it is operated. Staff appraisal meetings will take less time and be more productive if both parties prepare in advance and use standard preparatory forms.

(p 118)   Have a sound system of personal development plans operating in your department. This will involve every member of staff in the development process, save you some time and is an effective and efficient system.

(p 134)   Prepare lesson plans for all sessions that you present on a regular basis, adding in details of aids, questions and timings, etc.

Time Saving

The constant battle for most managers is getting the most out of their time. The purpose of all the speedtraining tips is to help with that. Those that are particularly important for saving time are listed below:

(p 38)   Always try to use available information, forms or systems before producing new specifications.

(p 43)   Refer to existing job descriptions and person specifications produced by the personnel department to help you determine experienced worker standards.

(p 54)   Use in-house training staff to carry out a range of tasks on your behalf.

(p 56)   Make full use of an effective time-planning/time-management system.

(p 59)   Always adapt existing documents to meet your needs where possible.

(p 90)   Hold a half-day meeting twice a year with key staff to discuss and identify training needs that are likely to emerge over the next six months.

These tips are described in more detail in other sections of the index.

Training Department

While this book is for managers, it is appropriate to highlight those tips which refer to the training department since it is good management practice to get the most out of whatever specialist resources are available. The most relevant tips are listed below.

(p 54)   Remember the importance of harnessing the skills of a training department where one exists.

(p 59)   Find out and use what is easily available in the training department in the form of documents.

(p 125)   Use or modify training materials which may be available from a training department to plan and deliver your own training sessions.

(p 146)   Use standard forms produced by the training department, if any exist, to help evaluate your own training sessions.

Appendix 2:
The Role and Contribution of Training and Development in the Management of Change

Appendix 2:
The Role and Contribution of Training and Development in the Management of Change

It seems to me that the evidence of everyday experience fails to support a notion that individuals naturally or by definition resist change. All of us embrace many changes in our lives. Some of these are fairly minor and of relatively little consequence – a new hairstyle, a mode of dress, or a new car. Others such as moving house, getting married or changing job or career are more important and are pursued with perhaps more thought. Once a decision to change is taken, it usually generates a high degree of commitment and enthusiasm. Yet other changes are even more significant in a person's life and involve a reappraisal of beliefs and values, for example getting divorced, changing religion or switching political allegiance. Even these fundamental changes are not resisted just for the sake of it though equally they are not likely to be embraced lightly.

Essential Conditions

There are, I believe, two conditions inherent in all these changes experienced by individuals which determine and create lack of resistance and produce commitment. The first is that they are in the control of the individual; they result as a consequence of a personal decision. The second is that individuals expect beneficial outcomes; that is, they believe embracing the change will make their lives better, happier, or more satisfying. The lesson seems to be that change will be embraced by individuals in organizations if those conditions are present.

An amusing way of representing one of these conditions is contained in the following formula:

Change happens when AB + CD > EF and GH

where

AB = Alternative Benefits;
CD = Current Dissatisfaction;
> Is greater than;
EF = Energy Forecast;
GH = General Hassle.

What is being said is that change will be embraced if it is perceived as being likely to bring about an improvement which is worth the cost of achieving it. What it also implies is that the decision to change or not is a personal one and therefore there is implicit support for the first condition – individual control, as well as the second – beneficial outcomes.

Applying the Conditions to Organizations

Applying this argument to organization change, it seems that there are only four reasons why individual members do not embrace change:

1. They do not have the ability.
2. They do not know of the change.
3. They do not believe the change.
4. They do not agree with the change.

The first is obviously a straightforward training and development issue, which will be examined in more detail in the next section. The second is a too-common reason in organizations. Often managers make decisions and adopt policies or strategies that require individuals to behave differently. These are either not communicated at all or done so ineffectively, with the result that staff continue to behave in the established way and fail to adopt new behaviours simply because they are unaware of a requirement to change. The third reason is also not uncommon. Communication in terms of transmitting the information is effective but staff do not believe that the organization really desires the change. The feeling is that managers are not really serious and are simply 'going through the motions' or 'paying lip-service' to some new fashionable concept or legal requirement.

Some examples of these two reasons operating in practice may be helpful. I was once asked to provide some management training for junior managers in an organization that was subject to increasing competition and was performing ineffectively in response. Prior to the changed market situation the organization had enjoyed relatively easy success and therefore had adopted a fairly lax approach to cost control. There was a need now for a much more cost-conscious approach to the work and effective operation of cost-control procedures. Perhaps I was naïve but I was amazed to discover that the junior managers did not know of the market conditions or the organization's poor performance. The planned training became something of an irrelevance once that situation was rectified.

Many organizations have experienced failure in trying to implement concepts such as team briefing or total quality management (TQM). The same is even more true of taking on legislative requirements such as health and safety procedures or, to take a UK example, the Data Protection Act. In these cases members of staff are required to behave differently, ie, they have to change the way they do their jobs. The fact that they do not is often explained by a disbelief in the organization's commitment to the change. While they know of the change individuals do not believe that they are really required to adopt it by the organization. It is in overcoming this reason that the old adage 'actions speak louder than words' is never more true. Staff take their cues from what managers actually do rather than what they say.

The fourth reason simply reflects the two conditions described earlier. In order for individuals to adopt a change and be committed to it they have to feel some control over the decision to change and be convinced of some beneficial outcomes. The first of these conditions is not necessarily true in all cases if the second is clearly present. This is particularly the case if the change does not impact on personal beliefs and attitudes. Generally, change is more likely to be adopted if individuals are *involved* in decision making.

The nature of this involvement can vary depending on the nature of the change. If it is of minor significance, for example similar in personal terms to changing one's hairstyle, then the involvement can remain at an intellectual level. If it is of major significance, for example similar in personal terms to changing one's religion, then the involvement has to include examination of beliefs and values. Involvement also has the benefit of dealing with the other reasons for non-adoption of change. If individuals are involved they will know of the change and believe managers are serious about it as well as being more likely to agree with it.

The Overall Contribution of Training and Development

Training and development has a number of contributions to make to the management of change. First, and perhaps most critical, is to ensure that the 'people' issues and implications of change are raised and understood. Failure to do this is often a reason why planned change does not work or why organizations respond too late or ineffectively to environmental change.

A second contribution lies in helping individuals to develop their ability to cope with change itself. Personal development programmes and team development activities can be designed to build the coping skills required to live easily with the ambiguity and uncertainty which invariably accompany change. I find it useful to do this by focusing on the life experiences of individuals and encouraging them to examine personal changes such as those identified earlier, for example, getting married and becoming a parent. Such programmes can also encourage risk taking by allowing for experiment in a supportive climate. Being able to take risks in situations of uncertainty is useful, if not essential, in coping with and managing change.

Management development provides opportunities for a third contribution. Programmes can have those items identified in the last paragraph as a major theme. They should always, in my view, enable managers to fulfil their responsibilities for developing their own staff. Managing the learning process as it occurs in doing work is an essential component of a learning organization. This requires managers who are effective developers of people. Training can also help managers in this through appropriate support mechanisms and materials.

The fourth contribution can also form part of management development but has wider application. It is simply providing knowledge and skills in utilizing change processes. Appropriate training can develop in managers at all levels the knowledge and skill required to gain commitment to change – an essential ingredient in managing change. Trainers can also provide direct consultancy and advisory services on applying change processes in particular contexts. As part of this, provision of training activities can make a contribution to overcoming the three barriers of knowing, believing and agreeing.

The fourth barrier of ability leads to a fifth and perhaps most obvious contribution. It is often the case that a specific change will create a need for new knowledge and skills to be available within the organization and to enable individuals to continue to perform effectively. Training and development contributes here through diagnosing training needs and implementing appropriate strategies to meet them. The management of change can never be complete or effective unless arrangements exist to develop the necessary ability to meet the consequences of a given change.

There is a sixth and equally important contribution. It is to encourage and enable individuals and teams to both regularly review their current performance and to raise their heads above the parapet to survey the operating environment. Trainers are well placed to facilitate open discussion on performance, to contribute expertise in helping to diagnose causes of poor performance and to help identify where and how improvements are possible. Unless such activities take place regularly, downward trends in performance may only be identified when it is too difficult to reverse them. Internal change in response to the environment can only be managed effectively if external change is identified early enough and responses planned in advance. Training has a key part to play in developing an outward-looking and future-oriented approach to managing the organization. Such an approach requires that time is devoted to examining and analysing significant features of the operating environment.

These six contributions represent a summary of what is possible. No doubt they can be added to. The contents of this book will hopefully enable those contributions I have identified to be made.

Further Reading
from Kogan Page

APL: A Practical Guide for Professionals
Susan Simosko

Assessment Management Skills
A Guide to Competencies and Evaluation Techniques
Margaret Dale and Paul Iles

British Qualifications
(23rd Edition)

Coaching, Mentoring and Assessing
A Practical Guide to Developing Competence
Eric Parsloe

Competence-Based Assessment Techniques
Shirley Fletcher

Competency-Based Human Resource Management
Value-Driven Strategies for Recruitment, Development
and Reward
*Edited by Alain Mitrani, Murray M Dalziel and David
Fitt*

Cost-Effective Training
A Manager's Guide
Tony Newby

Designing Competence-Based Training
Shirley Fletcher

Develop Your Management Potential
A Self-Help Guide (Second Edition)
Charlotte Chambers, John Beech, John Coopey and Adrian McLean

Developing Management Skills
Techniques for Improving Learning and Performance
Margaret Dale

Effective Decision Making
A Practical Guide for Management
Helga Drummond

Effective Performance Management
A Strategic Guide to Getting the Best from People
John Lockett

Evaluation: Relating Training to Business Performance
Terence Jackson

Handbook of Training Evaluation and Measurement Methods
(Second Edition)
Jack J Phillips

Handbook of Training Management
Kenneth Robinson

How to Be a Good Judge of Character
Methods of Assessing Ability and Personality
D Mackenzie Davy

How to Be an Even Better Manager
(Third Edition)
Michael Armstrong

How to Design and Introduce an Appraisal Training System
Carol McCallum

How to Develop and Present Staff Training Courses
Peter Sheal

How to Take a Training Audit
Michael Applegarth

Human Resource Management
Strategy and Action
Michael Armstrong

The Lone Trainer
How to Set Up the Training Function Singlehanded
Mike Saunders and Keith Holdaway

Managing Change Through Training and Development
Jim Stewart

Managing Training
Sunny Stout

Measuring Management Performance
A Developmental Approach for Trainers and Consultants
Terence Jackson

Not Bosses But Leaders
John Adair

NVQs, Standards and Competence
A Practical Guide for Employers, Managers and Trainers
Shirley Fletcher

One-to-One Training and Coaching Skills
Roger Buckley and Jim Caple

A Practical Approach to Group Training
David Leigh

A Practical Guide to Project Management
How to Make it Work in Your Organisation
Celia Burton and Norma Michael

Personnel Administration Manual
Chris Warren

Readymade Business Forms
Michael Armstrong

The Recruitment Workbook
Stan Crabtree

The Staff Development Handbook
An Action Guide for Managers and Supervisors
Peter Sheal

Successful Induction
How to Get the Most From Your New Employees
Judy Skeats

The Talent Factor
Key Strategies for Recruiting and Retaining Top Performers
Terry Lunn

The Theory and Practice of Training
Roger Buckley and Jim Caple

The Trainer's Desk Reference
(Second Edition)
Geoffrey Moss

Training for the Small Business
Jenny Barnett and Liz Graham

Training for Total Quality Management
Bill Evans, Peter Reynolds and Dave Jeffries

Training Needs Analysis in the Workplace
Robyn Peterson

For further information on these and other Kogan Page titles please contact our Customer Service Department at:

Kogan Page Ltd
120 Pentonville Road
London N1 9JN
Tel: 071 278 0433 Fax: 071 837 6348